Soldiers of God

by
douglas scaddan

Soldiers of God

Scaddan Publishing

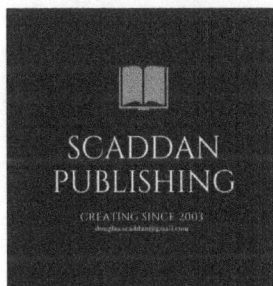

SCADDAN
PUBLISHING

CREATING SINCE 2003
douglas.scaddan@gmail.com

Soldiers of God Copyright © 2020 Douglas Scaddan

Published by Scaddan Publishing

ISBN: 978-0-9683071-8-2

Praise for The Trustee's Manual

The author's knowledge and application of scriptures makes The Trustee's Manuel indispensable for basic trustee training. His experience and research enables an informed presentation delivered in an engaging style. Purposefully, he removes lingering doubts about the spiritual role of Christians entrusted with civic stewardship on behalf of congregations. Believers will be able to grasp the essential role of trustee without feeling the need to be a bible scholar. I highly recommend this gem.

- Samuel (Amazon.com user)

Praise for The Janitor

This book may be a work of fiction, but the voice of Scaddan's narrative makes it feel as real as my own life. I was challenged by this book, reintroduced to the love of God and simple faith, and filled with tears as I related to the pains and joys of my new friends off these pages. I recommend this book to anyone who can spare a few minutes for a short read.

    - Josh (Amazon.ca user)

Dedication

To those that sacrifice.

Yet ask for nothing in return.

Acknowledgments

Kieran Ballah
Jim Barris
Freddy Blackstone
Scott Graves
Ben Trafford

Also by Douglas Scaddan

The Janitor
The Trustee's Handbook
The Lightbringer

PART ONE

DOUGLAS SCADDAN

PROLOGUE

He woke up, choking the scream into a barely audible grunt. His hand reached under the pillow for the handgun that wasn't there, and rolling out of the bed to crouch behind it, facing the window. He turned his head, the smell of gunpowder and burning flesh wasn't there. The soft, clean breeze that came through the open window carried the sweet smells of spring. Rolling out of the bed he stood and held his breath to listen, no gunfire, no explosions, no screaming. For a moment he had to concentrate on where he was. The angle of the streetlights through the open window told him he was on the second floor of a house, his house. The memories came crashing in, he was safe. He was alive. He was not injured.

He lifted his wrist and automatically shielded the watch-face as he pushed the indiglo button. 4:36 AM. Looking down at his bed the sheets were a tangled mess. His pillow was soaked with sweat and the lamp on the bedside table was on the floor. He shook his head, absently placing the lamp back in its, place on the bedside table, and wandered down to the kitchen. Sitting at the table he stared sullenly at the space between the wall and himself. After a moment, the first desperate shudder of his big shoulders brought his head hanging down towards the table. A second later the tears came, and he knew that shortly the ach in his stomach would rise and turn into an emptiness that would deprive him of air, and thought as he descended into fear. Gideon Steele laid his head on the table and wept.

*

The next morning Gideon sat in a wicker rocking chair sipping a cup of steaming Earl Grey tea from a porcelain tea cup, his hand slightly trembling. Beside him on a side table sat a matching pot and a second cup and saucer. He watched as kids started coming from the houses and making their way to the end of the cul-de-sac towards the school at the end of Landsmere court. Mrs. Gable stood from where she was weeding her garden and waved. He raised his cup in salute and smiled to her.

Forest Hills was a small community of only around two thousand people. To the north-east, along Highway 6 lay the town of Fergus. To the south, along the same highway that ran through the middle of town lay the

1

larger "Twin Cities" of Kitchener\Waterloo, where most people from Forest Hills went to shop. Directly west along a little used county road was the small village of Dunnville, which only boasted a convenience store, a hardware store, a Tim Horton's and a small church that operated out of a movie theatre that had been closed. Gideon had deliberately chosen Forest Hills because it was small, but close enough to other towns that he could find something, if Forest Hills didn't have it.

A blue mini-van rolled down the street and stopped in front of his house. The man that got out of the van was tall and thin, his short, balding brown hair was, as yet, untouched by grey, but his brown eyes were bright and sharp. He approached the steps to the porch and smiled as he stood, with one foot on the bottom one.

"So, Mr. Steele, I see you have absolutely nothing to do on a beautiful, Tuesday morning, " he said, with a smile.

"One of the great benefits of being retired," Gideon replied.

The man at the bottom of his steps was Pastor Chris Taylor, the senior pastor of the Forest Hills Church of God, the small neighborhood church up the street.

Gideon Steele, stood from the wicker chair, set his teacup on the side table and took a couple steps to the top of the stairs. His long, thick arm reached down and engulfed Chris' hand in one of his meaty palms as he smiled.

"You're only 44, Gid." Chris laughed.

Gideon smiled. "I've put a lot of miles on this old body!"

Chris got to the top of the porch and sat in an identical wicker chair.

The chairs creaked as the two rocked back and forth, Gideon had been gifted them by his parents when he had retired from the Military, and decided to buy a house. They had always sat on his parent's front porch, now they sat on his. His Dad had told him that they were once his grandparents, many years of care, repairs and love had kept them in tact through the years.

"And yet you're still in better shape than any guy half your age." Chris remarked.

Three years ago Gideon had retired from the military as a Captain, and Special Forces assault specialist. He collected a pension that allowed him the freedom to not work and he was still young enough that he could keep

2

himself in excellent shape. It was on one of his morning runs that he had met Chris, who was out in the yard trying to cut down a small tree. Gideon stopped and helped him, feeling sorry for the way he was awkwardly swinging the axe.

Chris had invited him in for coffee and Gideon found himself sharing with this small, mousy, pastor things that would have horrified him to share with the members of his old squad. Fears, nightmares, stories that still bubbled to the surface years after they had happened, which left him crying and alone at his kitchen table in the middle of the night. Chris sat there sipping his mug of coffee and taking it all in.

When Gideon had left, he stood at the door and shook Chris' hand, as Chris invited him to Forest Hills Church of God, where he was the pastor.

"Clean living and a pastor that comes by two or three mornings a week to make sure I'm being good." Gideon poured Chris a cup of tea and handed him the cup and saucer.

"Why do you use these things?" Chris asked lifting his cup. His eyes narrowed slightly at the shake in Gideon's normally rock solid hand and the dark rings around his eyes.

"My Mom always told me that coffee mugs are for coffee and teacups are for tea. Everything has a purpose and to use it for anything else is just silly." Gideon replied mimicking his mother's voice.

Chris laughed and took a sip from the delicate cup. "Well if your Mom says so." Chris looked at the fine hand painted flowers on the sides of the cup. "Where did you get these anyways?" He added.

"They were my grandmother's. Mom gave them to me after I retired from the military, these chairs are from them too. I still remember Gramma pulling them out every Sunday when we'd go there for dinner. Tea at four, dinner at six." Gideon waved to one of the parents as he walked his kids to school. A long moment of silence passed.

"I wanted to ask you if you'd help out with something at the church," Chris said in guarded, too casual tones. "The Church of God in Canada is sponsoring a Christian Survival camp for the youth during one week in August."

Gideon set the teacup down suddenly, knowing where Chris was leading, he feared he might drop it.

"Our insurance requires that we have one person certified in wilderness survival with us. I assume that it was part of your training?" Chris made it sound like it was just a casual conversation, knowing full well that Gideon had avoided working with the youth in the church.

Gideon nodded watching Mrs. Gable pull out the hose from her garage to water her garden, thankful for something else to look at. Chris made it sound like it was just a casual conversation, knowing full well that Gideon had avoided working with the youth in the church.

"It's just for a week and you'd simply be in charge of the safety of the youth and the counselors. Making sure that we all know how to make a fire, or that kind of thing." Chris added, also watching Mrs. Gable but keeping a watch on Gideon's body language.

Gideon lifted the cup again, drained it, poured another, and held it in his hands as he looked down into the dark liquid. What do I do, Lord? He asked. He sat for a moment, just staring at the tea. Small ripples appeared in the liquid, his hand was shaking again. He set the cup down with deliberate care.

That day at Chris' front door had started a journey for Gideon, one that started at Chris' coffee table and ended with his baptism five months later. Gideon would join small groups and sign up for newsletters. His appetite for books was bottomless, and he attended every seminar or special event that came to the area.

The youth in the church were fascinated by this large six foot, three inch man with the big toned muscles and the bald head. They constantly wanted him to join in their youth events, campfires or worship services. Gideon turned them down every time, though he loved to hear the youth leaders talk about how well the group was doing or what the plans were for the future.

Gideon loved the young people, loved their life and the futures they looked forward to. They're hope was what he told himself he had fought for, but he felt like an outsider, like he came from another planet and that they wouldn't be able to understand what he said. His biggest fear was that they wouldn't understand why he had made the choices he had in his life. How could he possibly make them understand the things he had experienced so that the young people didn't make the same mistakes?

"What kind of challenges will there be for the kids?" He asked, forcing his voice steady.

Chris was surprised by the sudden question. "What do you mean?"

"Well is your purpose to actually teach them some survival techniques or just to make a site and sit there studying the Bible for a week?"

"We hadn't really planned that part yet." Chris admitted sheepishly.

"Well you've only got three months, better get to it," Gideon said, dryly.

"Can I count on your help?" Chris asked.

"You can always count on me, Chris," Gideon said with a wry smile, "just don't count on me to change those kids lives. That's your job."

"Ask yourself this, Gid, what is the measure of a man?" Chris said, softly. "I don't think we've seen your full measure yet. There's so much more to you and I think you'd be surprised with it yourself. You have so much to offer these kids that are still learning to be adults, and here you are. You've been around the block a few times and you've lived to tell about the dangers in the world.

"I'm not asking you to change their lives, Gid. I'm asking you to be you and maybe, just maybe being you will help one of those kids decide who he, or she, is."

Gideon nodded. "We'll see." He smiled almost sadly. "Anyways where is this little trip going to?"

"Just south of Lion Rock, about five hundred kilometres north of here."

"Isn't that the rock that new climbers practice on?"

"Yes, I believe so, why?"

"Might be a good challenge." Gideon replied with a grin.

"It'll give the Board of Directors a collective apoplexy!" Chris laughed.

Gideon nodded. "That'll be fun too," He said, with a straight face.

Gideon and Chris spent the next hour forming out a list of challenges for the youth to face as they were on their retreat. Fire starting, woodsman ship skills, basic tracking and rock climbing were all on the list. Rope work, finding and erecting shelters, how to find food and what could be eaten were added when Gideon mentioned they should only bring what they could carry on their backs.

Chris was amazed at how much of these skills his friend knew from first-hand knowledge, and Gideon would regularly say things like, "When I was in . . ." or "I knew a guy that taught me . . ."

When they were done they had a basic schedule of events and a general idea of how much it would cost. Chris stepped down off the porch and shook Gideon's hand.

"I'm glad you're helping us, Gid."

"All I've done so far is agree to make a list with you. I'll train your adult counselors and if you still need a guy for insurance I know enough guys that'll help you." Gideon replied staring at his lap. "I haven't actually agreed to anything yet."

"That's enough for now." Chris said as he turned to his van.

Once Chris was gone, Gideon tidied up the tea cups and pot and brought them into the house. As he washed them, he stared out at his backyard.

The youth terrified him. It was the idea that he might have some sort of influence on their lives. He had made so many mistakes in his that Gideon felt he was a bad role model for anyone, let alone young adults. Those kids would be looking to him as a leader, someone that they should emulate and Gideon was sure that he would fall far short of the mark.

His mind flashed to the vision of a small girl approaching a barricade he was guarding with a couple other men. They had repeatedly told her to stop. His eyes flashed on a wrapped bundle she was carrying and the smile on her face. Someone yelled, "Bomb!", a well placed shot to her forehead, and a doll rolled out from a threadbare blanket.

How could Gideon, who had spent more than half his life in violence, teach youth to be adults? Gideon, himself had not even been anything that could be called a youth. How would they ever be able to relate to him? How could the trust him? His mind flashed again to the vision of a doll rolling on the dirt.

Straight out of high school, Gideon joined the military and showed an aptitude for firearms. He repeatedly scored high in all the tests and was welcomed with open arms into the assault specialist training course, where he easily excelled beyond everyone's expectations.

When asked about joining Special Forces, Gideon jumped at the chance for action, being a mere twenty years old, he was still young and moldable, a perfect soldier. Once that training was over the real world took a hold of him, chewed Gideon up and spat him out. Years of missions, and killing turned him into a decorated combat veteran, but he was empty inside.

A great hole replaced his heart, a festering wound that grew larger and more painful with every death. It became harder and harder to return to the world of the "normal" Canadian, and he found himself staying in his small rented apartment in Toronto and staring at the walls around him, reliving every moment of every mission, again, and again, and again.

He became obsessed with becoming the perfect soldier, endurance training, strength training and taking three different martial arts all during his off hours, he excelled at everything, but with every death by his hand, the hold got deeper, the pain greater.

Shortly after his fortieth birthday he told his Commanding Officer that he wanted to retire. He was talked into one last mission. Ten men went in to retrieve a person that was being held against their will, a Canadian that was kidnapped in some country that Gideon had forgotten. Gideon, his Commanding Officer and the civilian were the only people to return.

Gideon retired after that. There were no arguments that could keep him there.

Looking down at his hands Gideon realized he had been washing his hands, over and over, turning them around each other in the soapy water. He picked up the other cup and started cleaning it.

But how should he react to Chris' question? 'What is the measure of a man?' What was it that made Gideon a man of God and what were the things he had to offer? The answer to that question was far more complex than it seemed. Who was Gideon Steele?

When he had finished cleaning the dishes he went down to the basement where he had set up a small gym, complete with weights, a treadmill and a heavy bag. Slipping on the thinly padded training gloves and fastening them tightly around his wrists he took a few sharp punches at the bag.

Soon he had developed a rhythm that brought sweat out onto his brow. Who was Gideon Steele? he asked himself with every punch. The chain rattled overhead and the ache in his stomach started up again.

For years he was Captain Gideon Steele, one of the best trained and most respected of the small brotherhood of Special Forces assault teams. He had trained with Navy Seals, and British SAS, and took everything they could teach him. He had formed his body and mind into a finely tuned killing machine, sure of himself and confident in his ability to attack anything head on. Until the mind that operated the machine fell into the deep pit in his chest. A man that had faced bullets, and bombs; a man that faced danger and death for a living was now reduced to a man whose hands shook with fear when asked to guide a bunch of teenagers on a camping trip.

He started a series of quick punches to where an opponent's midsection would be then went up to where the head would be and then back down. Over and over he did this, only realizing near the end that he was screaming with every punch. Long, screams from deep within his chest, with no meaning, that scratched his throat raw. Tears started rolling down his cheeks as frustration and anger filled his eyes. Each punch set the chain rattling and shook the big floor joist above his head.

When he stopped, he was panting hard and reached up to hold the chain and let his body hang on it. He rested his bald pate on the leather bag and sucked in air.

"Who am I?" Gideon said to no one.

He showered and went to the living room where he picked up a Bible. He looked up at a print of a painting of the face of Jesus by Akiane Kramarik and laughed.

"I know, I should have gone here first." Then Gideon opened the book.

*

Chris arrived home and stepped into the vestibule of the small duplex where he lived with his wife and two kids. Mary was four years old and at Kindergarten today, but Beth, the two year old was home and rushed as fast as her chubby legs could carry her to her father's leg where she latched on with a vice grip.

"Hi, Daddy!" She yelled at the top of her lungs, her long brown hair bobbing up and down as she tried to climb Chris' leg.

"Hi, Beth." Chris replied, picking up the small girl. "What's going on?"

"She's bored." Chris' wife Tina walked into the room from around the corner carrying a washcloth and a handful of crayons. "She decided the stairway needed redecorating." She set the crayons on the coffee table and handed the washcloth to Beth. Taking the girl in her arms Tina headed back towards the kitchen.

"Don't bother taking your shoes off, John wants to meet you at the church," Tina said. With her back to Chris he couldn't see her face but he could imagine the smile. She set Beth down and pointed to the 'redecorating' marks just out of Chris' view. "Clean."

"Did he say what he wanted?"

8

"He kept on asking when you'd be back from Gideon's" Tina frowned, she turned to face him. "Probably has to do with the camping thing then, right?" The ice in her tone was making the air cold.

Chris nodded. "Probably."

"You're still dead set on leaving us for a week to go, then?"

"It was my idea, baby," Chris said, reaching into his pocket for his cell phone. "I pretty much have to go."

"What you have to do is be a father to these girls," Tina said. "Set aside some time before and after the trip to spend with us."

"I have commitments to the church too." Chris replied calmly. "It's a calling and to ignore that would be against the will of God."

Tina walked over and set a hand on her hip. "I understand that. But your family is a calling too. You've been called to be a husband to me and a father to the girls. You need to make time for us too."

Chris leaned down to kiss his wife, but she stepped back. "I will. A week before or a week after."

Tina nodded and turned to walk back to where Beth was twirling the cloth over her head. Chris watched his wife for a moment. Tina had a lithe swimmer's body and blond hair to just past her shoulders. He watched her sway as she walked to the kitchen before she turned and looked at him.

"Were you just checking me out, Pastor Taylor?" She asked with a smile that Chris had learned to be careful around.

"I most certainly was, Mrs. Taylor." Chris replied with a cautious grin.

"We'll see what might happen a 'week before or a week after'." Tina nodded with a satisfied grin and took the cloth from Beth.

Chris stepped back out of the house and thumbed the speed dial for John Rogers, the Chairman of the Board of Directors for the Church of God in Canada.

"Chris?" John answered on the second ring. "Thanks for getting back to me so quick. I'm at the church now, can you come?"

"Be right there, John." Chris hung up and pulled the van back out of his driveway and into the street.

It was only a short drive to the church and he noticed John's car there as well as two other cars that surprised him. What's going on here?, he wondered. As he got out and headed to the front doors he saw John there with Sara Michaels and Dave Caldwell standing with the older man.

The three of them, plus Chris would mean that there was an "impromptu" meeting of the Church of God in Canada's Executive Committee. The only missing member would be John's older brother, who was recovering from knee replacement surgery.

John Rogers was an older man, perhaps eighty or eighty-five years, his thin, bony body and wrinkled face hid a mind that was as sharp as any twenty year old. He still boasted a full head of hair, albeit silver with age, and a firm grip. John had been serving as the Chairman of the Executive Committee for twenty years and while he had been a stable and firm leader, Chris was waiting for a younger, more modern leader to come along.

Sara Michaels was in her late thirties and had never married. She was a full time nurse at St. Mary's hospital in town and regularly worked in the ER. She had quick blue eyes that never missed anything, and a small delicate frame that made it seem impossible that she could withstand the stress and physical exertion of working in an ER. She smoothed an ankle length skirt and smiled as Chris locked his van.

Dave Caldwell was in his late forties and the pastor of the Church of God in Dunnville, the next town over. He was a slightly overweight man with thinning black hair and a constant frown that made one think he was smelling something bad. He peered at Chris through thick wire rimmed glasses and jammed his hands in the pockets of his corduroy suit coat.

The Church of God in Canada was, less than aptly named. There were only about forty churches in the organization, and most of them were in Ontario, with two in Quebec and one in Manitoba. The founders of the 'movement', as they liked to call it, were being proactive and expecting the Church of God to spread throughout Canada like wildfire. That was eighty years ago. It was spreading, but more like a snail carrying a log.

Chris walked up and shook each hand in turn before opening the church and turning off the alarm.

"Should we go upstairs to my office?" He asked.

Without waiting for an answer Chris led the way upstairs to his long, narrow room that Chris liked to call his "Quiet Space". The church building was young, perhaps twenty years old, built after the congregation had become too large for the old building, topping out at about two-hundred regular attendees. The congregation had dropped and then risen and then dropped again before settling where it was now, three-hundred and holding steady. The work and energy that Chris and the church leadership had placed in it easily made it the largest and healthiest of all the Church of God congregations in Canada.

After sitting behind his desk, Chris asked if he could get anybody something to drink. John and he had Coke, Sara asked for water and David declined. Chris had just popped the tab on his can when David spoke.

"What did Gideon say?" He asked.

"He said he'd be willing to help us, but he's nervous around youth, so he's a little reluctant." Chris took a drink. "I think he's just not used to hanging around with young people. He hasn't really had much contact with them."

"Well, if he accepts, that takes care of our insurance problem." John said, with a smile.

"He does think it's important to have a list of challenges for the kids, though." Chris added.

"Like what?" David asked.

"How to build a proper shelter, make a fire with no matches or lighter, and a rock climbing excursion," Chris said. "There are a couple more, what plants and roots are okay to eat, what's not, that kind of thing."

"Rock climbing?" Sara asked. "That's pretty dangerous isn't it?"

"I asked the same thing." Chris smiled. "He said the only danger is gravity. He's taught rappelling and climbing hundreds of times, on larger cliffs."

"And he'll be comfortable teaching it to youth?" David huffed. "I thought you said he was nervous around them?"

"I did." Chris replied looking at David directly. "Look, we need to understand that Gid's a combat veteran, none of us can even imagine the things he's seen or done. He struggles with making meaningful connections with people because of these experiences. I think I'm the only person he talks to, outside of his old army buddies, on a regular basis. But I also have faith that he'll do what needs to be done."

*

Gideon closed his Bible and looked at the spruce bookshelf on the wall beside the fireplace. Setting the Bible on the end table he stood and took a few steps to scan the spines of the books neatly arranged by size.

His finger stopped at the title he wanted. The Measure of a Man, by

Gene A. Getz. He opened the book and glanced at the inscription.

To Gideon,

You may not feel it now, but you have the foundation of a great man of God. I hope this helps you on your journey.

Pastor Chris Taylor

"That sly dog." Gideon muttered with a chuckle.

He scanned the first few pages until he found the list he was looking for. He had been reading the book of Timothy when he remembered this volume. In the letters to Timothy and Titus, Paul had listed twenty basic attributes that were important to be a strong man of God.

According to Getz the list was, overall spiritual maturity, above reproach, and the husband of one wife. Well Gideon wasn't married but if he were he was sure he'd be faithful to her. Temperate, prudent, respectable, hospitable, able to reach (able to communicate clearly and non-defensibly), not addicted to substance, not self-willed, not quick-tempered, not pugnacious or abusive, gentle, peaceable, free from the love of money, manages his own household well, loves what is good, just, devout, and self controlled.

Gideon sat down again with the book and thought about himself. He could safely say that he was some of these things. But that wasn't really the point was it, to be able to identify them in ones-self? He needed to know if other people saw them in him. Gideon was never good at self-reflection, he found it fake and just a way to make yourself feel good about mistakes you may have made in the past. The only way to know if he was a strong man of God, like he wanted to be was to find out what other people saw in him, and if need be, work on his shortcomings.

And the only way he was going to be able to do that was to help out with people. People like the youth and people that he may have to mentor. In situations like the camp that Chris had literally brought to his front door this morning.

He looked at the painting of Jesus again, the loving, caring face looking down at him from his eggshell white wall.

"You sure do have a sense of humour, don't you?" He muttered to the painting, fear once more mounting in his chest.

*

"I'm not convinced that Gideon is the right person to be in charge of this camp," David said, again.

They had been talking back and forth for the better part of an hour and the same statement came out of the same mouth each time.

"He won't be in charge of it," Sara said, again. "He'd just be the survival expert."

"And in a survival camp, that pretty much puts him in charge." David said.

John held a hand up. "Rather than talking about Gideon behind his back, why don't we see if we can get him here?" He turned to face Chris, who had already pulled out his cell phone.

"Hey, Gideon," Chris said, turning slightly in his seat, away from the others. "I'm here at the church with the Executive Committee and we were wondering if you could come down and talk with them about the Survival Camp thing?"

There was a slight pause, then Chris said goodbye and placed his phone back in the holster at his hip. He smiled briefly.

"He says he'll be right over, and he's ready to be measured."

*

Gideon walked the three blocks to the church and into the foyer. He heard some talking from upstairs and figured they were in the pastor's office. When he got to the top of the stairs he turned right and saw that Chris' door was open. He rapped on the wood frame.

All four eyes turned to him. He had met Sara before, she attended the church here, but he had never met John or David and he was used to the shocked looks when they saw his wide shoulders fill the doorway.

"Hi everybody," Gideon said, with a smile. He noticed that John, Sara and Chris smiled back, but David just sat there looking like someone had killed his dog.

There was a strange silence as Gideon walked to an empty seat that was placed a few feet to the left of Chris' desk. He lowered his large frame into it and placed his hands in his lap. "What can I help you with?"

"We were wanting to know what your plans would be with the camp?" David asked outright.

13

"I have no plans for the camp." Gideon replied. "My understanding is that the plans will be made and approved by the camp committee."

David leaned forward, placing his elbows onto his knees. "But you do have some things that you would like done, right?"

Gideon held David's gaze for a moment. He noticed the slight smile on his face and the way his brows were furrowed down, almost in anger. His breath was short and he sucked it in quickly through his nose.

"You don't like me very much do you?" Gideon said, quickly.

David sat up quickly, clearly not expecting this reply.

"No matter." Gideon continued. "There are probably a couple thousand people in the world that don't like me very much. You're pretty low on my priority list.

"I am neither politically correct, nor really quite worried about people that don't like me, so you can see where I'm willing to make statements like that. I'm an old soldier, I do what needs to be done when it needs doing, no matter what my own personal feelings." Gideon stood. "You called me here for one reason, to ask me one question. Will I put your children in 'danger'? The simple answer is yes, anytime you go into an unfamiliar situation, you're putting yourself in danger. Will I push these kids to do things that are outside of their comfort zone? Yes I will, and they will be stronger and more confidant for it. Will I support these kids in everything they do and in every challenge I give them? Yes one hundred percent. Will your kids come back with more self-confidence? Yes. Will they come back ready to take on any challenge that this world has for them? Yes. Do I care what you think? No.

"One of two things is going to happen here." Gideon continued. "Either you are going to let this thing run without me and risk no insurance from your provider, or you'll let me do what I feel that God is telling me to do with these kids and make them strong, confident young adults. That decision is not mine so, there's no need for me to waste any more of your, or my, time."

Gideon stood and strode out of the room in three, long steps.

They sat, silent for a moment. David suddenly broke the silence. "I think he's perfect."

*

Gideon stood by the corner of the church, leaning heavily against the wall, resting his head on the brickwork. He was panting, he didn't want to think he was hyperventilating, but he was doing a very good impression of it. He was pleased that he had made it through his little speech without breaking apart. He knew that they wanted a confident man to lead the survival side of things, and Gideon needed to prove to himself, more than anyone that he was still confident. That he could still do what needed doing.

Taking one deep breath he pushed up from the wall and started home. Assault 101, Gideon thought. When in doubt attack.

An hour and a half later, Gideon sat in his living room leafing through a book. He wasn't even sure what the book was about, but he was just using it as something to occupy his hands. He had received the call shortly after he returned home. The board had decided that he would be totally responsible for the training of the other group leaders for the trip as well as the safety of the youth that were going on the trip. His mind raced with ideas. He was sure he'd need at least four weekends to properly train the leaders, and for that he would need help.

He suddenly stood up and dropped the book on the couch. Running up the stairs two at a time he burst into his den and sat at the corner desk. Reaching into a side drawer he pulled out an old, battered address book.

He checked a few pages, many of the names had been crossed out with a red pen, Too many, he thought. Gideon dialed a number on the phone that sat on the corner of the desk, an older model with the receiver still attached to the base by a cord. After a couple rings a deep, gravelly voice answered.

"Hello?" Gideon smiled. He could just picture his old friend, and comrade, Jim Barris standing in his doorway staring out at the fields full of sheep in northern Quebec.

"Ox?" Gideon replied. "It's Gideon, I need a favour."

"When and where, sir." The man called Ox replied. "I'll be there."

Gideon smiled. Jim Barris was one of the original 6 that had been on his assault team. He was a solid soldier and one of the biggest men that Gideon had ever met, standing over 6'7" and weighing in at almost 275lbs, "Ox" was, without a doubt, an imposing figure of a man.

"How soon can you make it to my place?" Gideon asked.

"Just as soon as I can get someone to watch my sheep," Barris replied. "What's up?"

"Need some help to train some people for a church youth camp trip.

15

Just basic survival stuff, nothing fancy. I'm on a time line, though."

Barris chuckled. "I haven't had a vacation in a couple years. Should be fun."

"Just remember we're not training soldiers here," Gideon said, with a chuckle. "These are church folk."

"Understood, Cap," Ox said, with a grin, "No teaching the church folk to kill."

ONE

Jerry Price was standing in front of the Lifestyles Editor of the Star, the biggest newspaper in Forest Hills. The editor's red face smiled up at Jerry. Too much coffee, not enough sleep and a diet that consisted mostly of fast food and doughnuts were starting to take its toll on his body. Kyle Borden will not be much longer in this world, Jerry thought.

"I want you to do a piece on the youth camping trip that's happening this summer, it's being put on by the Church of God in Canada but it's being pretty much run by the Forest Glen Church of God." the editor said.

"It sounds like a fluff piece at best." Jerry replied. "We getting that desperate for local interest stories?" he added with a laugh.

"It's a youth survival camping trip, Jerry, they're not even bringing tents, just what they can carry. The guy they just got to be their survival expert is ex-military. There's got to be a story there alone. Why did he join a church? Is he a pacifist now? How does he feel about his years of service?" Kyle smiled. "You can always find a story."

"My sister-in-law goes to that church. I can ask her what she knows," Jerry said. "I don't think it'll be too interesting though, a bunch of kids singing Kum Ba Ya around a fire." He added with a frown.

Kyle looked doubtful for a moment. "See where it leads. If anything you can do the 'Local guy serves his Country' angle. Guy's name is Gideon Steele."

"I've got some friends in Ottawa, maybe I can get his file," Jerry said. "Still sounds like a fluff piece."

Kyle nodded. "Just run with it, see where it leads. If anything you'll have a great warm fuzzy piece to write."

Jerry smiled wryly and turned to exit the office, paused, and turned back to Kyle. "How big a story do you want?"

Kyle didn't look up from the file he was looking at. "If it's good enough, you're probably looking at a series. Maybe you could do some stuff on the kids after, and see if their lives have changed for the better."

*

17

Jerry forced himself to grin, this was going to be the most boring assignment ever. He was looking for the break that would take him out of this town and into the big papers in Toronto or Ottawa. Doing local interest stories in the town of Forest Hills was not going to help him do that, he was grateful for the opportunity that he had here, it had allowed him to sharpen his craft, write for quality, and get a good feel for the expectations of the field.

He had slaved for years to make it to the point where he was now, writing small bit stories that were printed in the lifestyles pages. He had contacts in Ottawa, a friend he went to university with that now worked in Parliament, a cousin that was a Command Officer in the military, maybe they could help him out here, but Jerry Price wanted the big stories, and he wasn't going to find them in the sleepy town of Forest Hills.

He got to his desk and called his sister-in-law and found out that Gideon Steele was a big, quiet man that was always willing to help out in the church. He rarely said anything to anyone, but she knew that he was retired, she also thought he was someone important because he had worn his uniform to service on Remembrance Day last year, and he had a chest full of medals and ribbons. Jerry asked her what the badge on his shoulder looked like and she had to think for a moment.

"It had a red circle with a knife pointed up, I think," she replied.

Jerry froze for a moment. "Are you sure?" he asked. The symbol tickled something in his memory, he'd have to remember to dig for that later.

"Yep, I remember now thinking it was kind of plain, just a red circle, there were gold leaves and stuff at the bottom and a crown at the top, but the middle was kind of plain."

Jerry thanked her and smiled. After some digging online, Jerry discovered that the badge she had described was for the Canadian Special Operations Forces Command Unit. If this Steele guy was in that unit, this story just got a little more interesting. He would like to have confirmed everything with his cousin, but he hadn't talked to him in about a year, so he hoped he could get somewhere with his friend that worked on Parliament Hill with the Governor General.

*

Kieran James was sitting at his desk when the call came. He stared at the phone in frustration for a moment and then picked it up. Kieran was athletic, despite having a job that demanded long hours, constant travel and a lot of time behind a desk, he managed to put in time in the gym three or four times a week.

"James.", he said, tersely.

"Hi, Kieran, it's Jerry Price calling from Forest Hills," the voice on the other side was familiar to Kieran, his old roommate from the University of Toronto. Jerry had studied journalism and Kieran had studied law. He had kept in touch with Jerry by e-mail, and the occasional phone call, since he had moved to Ottawa to work for the Governor General.

"Hi, Jerry. To what do I owe this call at work?" Jerry had always called after hours, being a pretty big stickler for separating work, and friendship, the two had hardly ever discussed politics.

"I'm doing a story on an ex-military guy and I was wondering if you could help me out?" Jerry's voice was calm and professional. "Just want some background stuff. Local man serves country type thing."

"I have nothing to do with the Military, Jer." Kieran replied. He closed the document he was working on, and called up a military database that he had access to. "I can probably just give you the basics about him."

"Anything's better than what I have now. His name is Gideon Steele, he retired at least three years ago," Jerry said. "How's Tanya?"

Kieran winced, Tanya was his girlfriend from a couple weeks ago. She had since broken up with him, because his job kept him busy for days on end at times. "Let's not talk about Tanya right now."

"Sorry." Jerry winced too, he knew that Kieran had really liked her.

The screen on Keiran's computer filled with the standard form that he had expected to see. Gideon Steele's name was at the top, but every other bit of information, including his rank was filled with the word 'CLASSIFIED' in bold red letter

"Umm," Kieran started. He'd never encountered this before. "You're guy is classified. I can't even find out what his rank, birthday or hair colour is."

"You know any reason why he'd be classified from you?" Jerry was confused. He knew that Kieran had access to just about anything, and he also knew that if Kieran couldn't tell him anything he wouldn't. The thought of what would be classified from Kieran made Jerry curious.

"I can't really think of anything," Kieran said. "As far as I knew I have access to everything the Governor General does, and if it's restricted from me, then it's restricted from him, which means someone, somewhere is hiding something."

"I'm gonna call my cousin Mike," Jerry said. "He's the Special Operations Advisor for the Minister of Defense. Just wanted to call you first, since I haven't talked to Mike in about a year."

"Don't expect to get too much then, those guys are pretty tight lipped." Kieran chuckled as he flipped back to the document he was working on. "When you going to get down here for a round of golf?"

"Maybe when I learn how to putt." Jerry laughed.

"Yeah, see you never than." Kieran hung up the phone with a smile. Then frowned and stepped out of his office and walked the 30 feet to the Governor General's office. With a small rap on the door he opened it a few inches and stuck his head inside.

"Excuse me, sir. Do you have a minute?" Kieran asked.

Governor General Miles Doneven was a large, overweight man that loved heavy, rich food and expensive cigars. He looked up from a report he was examining and smiled at Kieran. His open door policy was simple, knock first and stick your head in, if Doneven wasn't alone, then apologize and step out.

"Come on in, Kieran." Doneven said in a raspy voice that sounded like a dying motorcycle. "What do you need?"

"I ran into a problem getting particulars for a retired soldier." Kieran started. "Every bit of data was classified, and denied from me."

Doneven frowned. He turned to his computer screen and clicked the mouse a few times. "Name?"

"Gideon Steele", Kieran said and sat down in the chair across from him.

After a few moments Doneven smiled. "Here he is." He pulled his reading glasses down and looked over them at the screen, suddenly the big man went pale and frowned. "Why did you want to know about him?"

"A friend of mine works at a paper in the town where this guy retired." Kieran explained, a little worried about why Doneven was pale. "He's doing a human interest story about him and how he served the country."

Doneven looked directly at Kieran and pulled his glasses right off. "My advice to you, son, is to tell your friend to find another vet to write about. Anyone but this guy."

Kieran stared at Doneven in shock. "What is it?" he asked.

20

Doneven shook his head. "I like you, Kieran. I really do, so I'm not going to tell you anything about Captain Gideon Steele and I'm going to forget you ever asked about him."

Kieran nodded and stood to leave the room, confused. Suddenly he paused and then continued out the door, hoping Doneven didn't notice the stutter in his step. He had never mentioned Steele's rank to Doneven.

*

Colonel Mike Stone was preparing a training competency report for the Minister of Defense when his phone rang.

"Colonel Stone speaking." He said in a clipped, tight voice.

"Hi, Mike. It's Jerry Price." Jerry hoped Mike would remember him.

Mike smiled and leaned back in his chair. "Cousin Jerry? What's it been, like a year?"

"Something like that," Jerry said. "Look, I hate to call and then ask for a favour, but I need some help tracking down a retired soldier I'm doing a human interest article on for the paper."

"No worries," Mike said. "Family is family. What's his name?" Mike turned back to his computer and pulled up his database program.

"Gideon Steele," Jerry said. "All I know is that he's retired."

Mike paused and turned away from his computer. "I know him, Jer," He said softly. "Drop it, cuz. No good is going to come from looking into this guy's history. Not for you, or for anyone else."

Jerry sighed and rubbed his eyes at his desk in Forest Hills. "Mike, who is this guy?" he sounded like he was begging. "I had a friend on the Hill look him up and he got nothing, not even a rank!"

Mike shook his head, even though he knew that Jerry couldn't see it. "He was a Captain, and he was a good soldier." Mike sighed and seemed to stare off into the past for a moment.

Jerry waited, holding his breath, praying that something else would come from the silence.

Mike suddenly blinked and came back to the present. "That's all I'll tell you, Jer. I'm sorry."

Jerry took a deep breath. "That's okay, Mike. National Security and all, right?"

"Something like that."

*

Kieran sat at his desk and stared at Gideon Steele's record, or lack thereof. The word 'CLASSIFIED' repeated over and over, and Doneven's sudden and irrational shutting down of any questions on the topic. He usually encouraged questions from all his staff, and Kieran, being with him almost all the time was used to Doneven sharing everything with him.

"I'm going to tell you everything, Kieran." Doneven had said on his first day. "I want you to be my second brain."

But being locked out like this was strange. Kieran felt, betrayed, un-trusted, and to a certain extent, hurt. He looked up to Doneven so much, and had respected him for so long, that the sudden change of character seemed so out of place that it made him think that something was being hidden, maybe it did have to do with National Security, but for six years Doneven had shared National Security secrets with him, and had even gotten him access to classified and secure documents. Never, had Doneven failed to explain something, or share something with him.

Kieran started to think that maybe, someone within the government was using the 'Classified Documents' label as a means to hide something. He also thought that maybe, Doneven was one of those people. He needed to find out what made Gideon Steele so special.

*

Sergeant Bailey was angry. He stood staring at the Corporal in front of him with fire in his eyes.

"What made you think it would be a good idea to leave classified documents on your cart as you went for lunch? How old are you, boy?"

"Momentary lapse, Sergeant. Won't happen again." The Corporal said. "I'm 21, Sergeant."

"At 21 years old you should be able to follow a simple rule like returning files before you go on lunch! And I know it won't happen again, 'cause if it does you'll be cleaning the latrines in some god-forsaken country the next day!"

The phone rang.

Bailey reached over and grabbed the phone. "Special Records," he growled.

"Hello, this is Kieran James from the Governor General's office, I'm looking for the jacket for a retired soldier." The voice on the other end was confidant and clear.

22

"Yes, sir. May I ask why you need the file?" Bailey wasn't going to get hijacked by not following procedure.

"No you may not," Kieran said, calmly.

Bailey winced and looked over at Mahoney, who was still standing at attention by his office door. If he passed this off to Mahoney, who was a world class screw up anyways, he would be able to deny any knowledge of anything that went wrong with this. The Governor General's office didn't just call up Special Records and request the jackets of retired soldiers. There was something wrong and it didn't sit right.

"Let me pass you off to one of our filers. He'll be able to help you." Bailey waved the Corporal over and handed the phone to him. "Just get the Spec-Op's name and call this guy back. I want my office back."

"Yes, Sergeant." The corporal replied.

"No files leave the building," Bailey said, sternly.

"Yes, Sergeant."

*

Kieran James sat at his desk and stared at the phone. The corporal he had spoken with said that all he had on Gideon Steele were some training records and a handful of commendations for combat action that there were no reports for. He had asked if that was strange and the corporal said it was illegal. Every combat action had to have an after action report in the file of each soldier that was involved in the action. The commanding officer of the unit had to write a report on every combat interaction for their unit.

It took some arguing with the corporal, but he finally agreed to make copies of the file and have them waiting for Kieran at the front desk of the records department. He asked about the rest of the unit that Steele was with and Mahoney said that he'd try to track them down, as well as the missing after action reports.

Kieran reached out and dialed Jerry Price's number. He leaned both elbows on his desk and held his forehead with one hand while he cradled the phone in the other.

Jerry answered on the third ring.

"Jerry, I think you should come up here and take me to dinner," Kieran said.

Jerry laughed. "I like you and all, Kieran, but . . ."

"Bring your notebook," Kieran said.

"I'll come down tomorrow evening and we can go to dinner, my treat," Jerry said, suddenly.

"I'm done at 4:30," Kieran said. I'll meet you at the Lucky Pheasant at 5."

"See you then." Jerry hung up the phone and smiled. This might just turn out to be a good story after all, he thought.

*

It was cool in Ottawa, cooler than it was in Forest Hills anyways. Jerry got off the small twin engine prop plane that he had been on for two hours. The flight wasn't bad and he had time to go over his notes from a brief phone interview he had managed to fit in with the pastor of the church that Gideon Steele attended.

The pastor had said stuff that Jerry was expecting. Gideon was always there and always willing to help out where he could. Gideon had spoken briefly about his time in the military but the pastor was pulling the Pastor slash congregant confidentiality thing and wouldn't go into detail about it.

All in all Pastor Chris Taylor seemed like a nice enough fellow that took his religion very seriously. He had mentioned that Gideon kept to himself mostly, rarely talked and never wanted to do anything that made him stand out.

Jerry didn't want to call Gideon Steele until he had some kind of background to play with. Something was special about this former soldier and Jerry wanted to know what.

Jerry hailed a taxi and checked that he had his return ticket for later that night. Jerry hated hotels and only felt comfortable sleeping in his bed, in his house.

"The Lucky Pheasant." Jerry said, with a smile at the cab driver.

The ride over to the restaurant was quiet. The cabby didn't even have the radio on. Jerry gazed out at the tall government buildings as they neared Parliament and he wondered, idly, if he would ever have the opportunity to work here. As dreams went Jerry knew he was aiming high, but for right now it was one story at a time, and there was a part of him that wondered where this story was going. Who was Gideon Steele? Why was he so hard to track down? What had he done for the military?

The car coasted to a stop and Jerry handed the driver fifty dollars for a forty dollar cab ride. Stepping out onto the sidewalk, Jerry adjusted his jacket and made sure the recorder was in his breast pocket and that his notebook was in his hand, then he stepped past the smoked glass doors of the Lucky Pheasant.

The first thing that Jerry noticed was the dimness of the room. Then the tangy smell of grilled meat and the bitter smell of beer. He looked around the room and saw Kieran sitting in a booth by the back doors that had a sign over top saying, "Washrooms". Stepping over he tilted his head and asked, "Something wrong with the window view?."

Kieran lifted his head and smiled, "Just wanted some privacy." He stood and gave Jerry a hug before sitting down and waving at a waiter.

Jerry sat down and the waiter came over and asked about drinks. Kieran just ordered a beer and he followed suit and ordered one too. Jerry placed his notepad on the table.

"What's going on, Kieran," Jerry said. "You look like a long tailed cat in a room full of rocking chairs."

"Doneven trusts me with everything," Kieran started. "He tells me everything, doesn't matter if he's supposed to or not, the guy lets me in on every thought, every decision and every bit of information he has. He calls me his Second Brain."

"Sounds like a good boss."

"I went to him about my getting stonewalled looking for this soldier of yours," Kieran continued, "he shut me down. Told me to let it go and advise you to drop it too."

Jerry nodded. "I know you. You didn't."

"My main thought is that Doneven, or other people inside the government may be using the classified label to hide illegal actions." Kieran whispered, leaning over the table.

"Do you have proof?" Jerry asked. He reached out and scribbled in his notebook.

Kieran shook his head. "No, but I found your guy."

"Nice." Jerry poised his pen over his notebook. "At least I've still got my fluff piece."

Kieran smiled crookedly. "No, you don't get it," he said. "Captain Steele is easily the scariest soldier I've ever read about."

Jerry leaned forward. "What do you mean?"

Kieran shook his head. "You need to know that my name goes nowhere near this and I will deny any knowledge of this conversation."

Jerry nodded. "Look, Kieran I will call you an unnamed source in the government." He leaned in even closer. "I will not let you fall, but I've still got to have some kind of documentation."

Kieran stared at Jerry, as if weighing him for a long time. "I've got copies of his training records and commendations in the car."

"Thank you," Jerry smiled.

Kieran nodded "Steele and his unit were so well trained and so good at what they did that the Canadian Government started hiring them out to other countries who couldn't take care of their own problems."

"But what was their job? What did they do?" Jerry was getting impatient.

"I'm not sure. Steele's file has commendations for combat related events but no corroborating after action reports, which my guy in records says is illegal." Kieran replied. "If I had to guess he was probably black ops. If a dictator needed killing they'd send these guys, if we needed the Colonel's secret KFC recipe, we'd send these guys. Just by reading about Steeles' training, these guys could probably do anything."

"What about the rest of his unit?" Jerry said.

Kieran shook his head. "I've got a guy tracking them down too, but no luck yet." Kieran held up his hand when Jerry went to say something. "No, I don't know their names. What I do know is his training; that was well documented. He's trained with everyone from SEALS, Mossad, British SAS, everybody. The guy you have down there is quite arguably the most dangerous man I've ever read about."

Jerry shook his head, speechless.

"Anyways, something went wrong somewhere because Steele broke down, PTSD his discharge report says. He retired and now is living in your quaint little town."

"Why are you telling me this, Kieran?" Jerry asked. His friend was generally a stickler for rules and he was breaking a few big ones just telling him about this stuff.

"Because there's more here than just Steele's missing reports," Kieran said. "Someone up there on the Hill is hiding something, and if it's illegal, I'm gonna find out what it is, and then I'm gonna send them to jail. Your story may be just in a small paper, but I guarantee that they'll find out about it, even if I have to show Doneven myself to get the ball rolling."

26

Jerry leaned back and took a deep breath. This was going to be the story of a lifetime, if he could get Steele to talk, it would be his crowning achievement. First he had to try to get an interview with the man. That would probably be harder than anything to get though. Kyle had told him he could do a series. If he painted Steele good in the first article, maybe he could get an interview for the second.

They spent dinner talking about Steele's training, what it meant and throwing around ideas of why he didn't have any after action reports, but yet, had combat commendations, and a slew of injury reports. By the time the bill came, Jerry placed his Visa on the tray and checked his watch.

"I've got a plane to catch," He said.

"Something is seriously wrong here," Kieran said. "I'm going to ask some questions and see if I can get any answers."

"Why are you so interested in this?" Jerry asked as he placed his card back in his wallet. "It's my job to be interested, why you?"

Kieran thought for a moment. "The government has a vast amount of authority." He mused. "It is, though, answerable to the people. I think that someone inside the government is abusing their authority. If they are, they're still answerable to the people."

*

Kyle Borden's eyes were getting wider and wider as he read the sheets of paper before him. Jerry was sitting in the chair opposite him with a look on his face, like a man waiting for his first born child.

"You have documentation for all this stuff?" Kyle asked.

"My source gave me copies of Steele's training reports and commendations." Jerry replied.

Kyle nodded. "I want those copied and put in our filing room downstairs. Someone is going to ask about this." He read it over a second time. "Have you spoken with Steele?"

Jerry shook his head. "I called him yesterday, he gave me the no comment thing."

Kyle nodded and stared at the article, reading it through and re-reading it. Checking each word and rolling the ideas around in his head until he was pretty sure what was going on. The article made Steele out to be a victim, a man that was used and then discarded by the military. It used the words 'black ops' a number of times in relation to the lack of after action reports in

Steele's file. The majority of it was concentrated on Steeles' training, since he had the documents to back it up.

The original idea of the church survival trip was placed at the end as almost an afterthought.

"You have evidence of his training. There is a question of why he was trained so effectively, but appears to have seen no action. I don't like the 'black ops' comments, it's a bit of a jump in logic. Cut them." Kyle smiled. "It's a good bit of journalism, though. Clean it up and get it back to me ASAP."

"You got it, Boss," Jerry said, moving away from the desk.

Kyle held up a hand. "Good work, Jerry," he said.

Jerry nodded and ran off to his desk to arrange his information and fire up his computer. He pulled up his piece and went through it word for word and sentence by sentence being critical with each bit. Did it fit, did it add to the information, but most of all he made sure that everything he even hinted at was backed up by the notes from the conversation with Kieran or the documents that he had gotten.

Once he had gone through the entire thing, he sat back, read it as a complete piece, and then went through it word for word again. He was his own worst critic and he knew that. That was what made him a good writer, he was able to look at everything he wrote and he expected it to be perfect. He went through it again, and then printed the final draft that he had for Kyle, running to his desk and slapping it into the inbox with a grin.

*

Kieran James stared at the file that was just shoved under the door of his office. He set his coffee cup down and looked around the room, as if someone was hiding behind the potted plant in the corner. He wasn't prone to paranoia, but there was something about this, missing files, classified soldiers and unknown folders being shoved under his door that made him want to look around for cameras. Did this stuff really happen in the real world, or just in movies?

It was late, Kieran's favourite time to go to the gym, but he was spending so much time looking for Gideon Steele that he had alot of his real work to catch up on. He'd had lunch with a Major that served as an aide to a Colonel that was an advisor for Special Operations to the Minister of Defense. The aide had said that on the evening that Kieran had dinner with

Jerry Price, the Minister of Defense, Doneven, and Colonel Matthew Yim, the Major's boss, had a closed doors meeting in the Minister of Defense's office. The Major hadn't heard much, but when Kieran mentioned that a friend of his was asking about a Captain Gideon Steele the man perked up and said that was one of the names that he heard.

This would normally not bother Kieran in the least. Technically the Governor General of Canada was the Commander-in-Chief of all Canadian Forces. This duty was ceremonial at best, and Kieran had sat in hundreds of meetings with the Minister of Defense as they arranged for tours of units in order to boost morale. The mention of Jerry's soldier though, and the fact that Kieran wasn't invited made him worry. If this was strictly a black-ops thing, Doneven wouldn't have been invited at all to sit in. If it had been a normal part of Doneven's job, Kieran would have been there, something was wrong.

A couple steps around his desk and he was staring down at the red folder sitting almost mockingly on the plush blue carpet. Kieran frowned, a red folder meant classified information. So the Minister of Defense and a Special Operations Colonel were involved in this now? Why was this man, and his military actions being hidden? How far did this go, and how many people were involved?

He carried the folder back to his desk and set it on the blotter. The folder was a couple inches thick, it would have had to have been forced under the door. Turning to the first page he saw a post it note on the inside cover.

Found the man you were looking for.
I'm done with this now.
Forget my name.
My advice to you, forget this guy's name too.
Annon

The pages in the folder were all red as well, to prevent copying. The first few pages were personnel files for five more soldiers, all listed as being in Steele's unit. All were KIA but one, Chief Warrant Officer James Barris, now living in Quebec raising sheep. Kieran smiled, thinking it was almost poetic, from a soldier to a shepherd. He turned the page and grinned.

"Bingo." Kieran hissed. The title of the first page read, "After Action Report".

TWO

Gideon sat in his wicker rocking chair holding the morning's Forest Hills Star, it had been one week, to the day, that he had agreed to help the church with the survival camping trip. His hands were shaking and the familiar tightness in his chest was increasing with each word he read. The details of his training were accurate, the author of the article, Jerry Price, claimed that he had documentation from an "undisclosed source in the government". At least the After Action Reports had not been found. That would have been disastrous.

The panic in Gideon's chest slowly melted and hardened into a burning anger. The article blamed nothing on him and made him out to be a hero, a paragon of military strength and training. What made Gideon angry was that he had spent the last three years of his life trying to distance himself from the violence and horrors that he had seen and committed in the name of National Security, and here it was, in black and white staring at him and every other citizen of Forest Hills.

The thought the occurred to him. What would happen with the survival week planned by the church? There was a short paragraph devoted to it and Gideon's involvement at the end of the article. The Church of God was vehemently pacifist in it's beliefs, what would the articles detailing of his training make them think of the man that went through that training? It was a bit of a touchy situation just to get him involved at all! What would the young people think? He knew that the people that knew his heart and his growing faith would back him, but what about the parents of the youth that didn't know him? What would they do?

Gideon sighed and closed his eyes. Lord, I need you. Lord I always need you, and I need your strength now more than ever. Please, Father, take this feeling of anger and fear from me, and let me be the strong man of God that you want me to be, he prayed. He promised that he would take on any problem that arose, one step at a time, oddly that was a process he learned in the military.

Chris' blue van pulled up and the young pastor paused a moment before exiting the vehicle. Gideon forced himself to smile and waved as Chris stepped up to the porch.

"Morning," Gideon said as he poured a second cup of tea.

"Morning," Chris replied, accepting the cup and sitting in the second chair. "Read the paper this morning?"

Gideon nodded, not trusting himself to speak.

"Tina wants to march down to the Star's office and force Price to print a retraction," Chris said with a laugh.

"I thought Tina didn't like the idea of you going away for a week on this trip?" Gideon asked. "It's the perfect opportunity for her to get it canceled."

Chris nodded. "She doesn't want me to go, but she knows your heart, and that's more important to her."

"Sorry about all this," Gideon said.

"No, need," Chris said, as he set his teacup back on the side table. "I read the article and I don't know if it's real or not, but I think I have a better idea of the things you might have done, or what you're capable of, anyways. I want you to know that whatever you used to do, that doesn't matter to me. What matters to me is what you do now, and I like that guy."

Gideon smiled and took a sip of his tea. "I was blessed to have a lot of good guys to get me through a lot of tough stuff. I'm still blessed to have at least two good friends who see me as I am, not as I was."

There was a moment of silence as Chris watched Gideon's face darken from some unspoken memory. "We need to talk about what's going to happen tonight," Chris said, softly.

"What's going to happen tonight?" Gideon asked, setting his teacup down and clasping his shaking hands in his lap.

"The board and some concerned parents want to meet with you tonight," Chris said.

Gideon nodded. "I figured they would. What time?"

"Seven o'clock at the church," Chris said. "It's just a question and answer session, no decisions will be made tonight."

"I have to get Ox in a few minutes." Gideon replied without looking up. "Who's Ox?"

"Jim Barris he's one of the original six in my unit. He's gonna help me train the counselors for the youth camp."

"We need to talk about tonight," Chris said, again.

32

Gideon turned a sad smile at Chris. "You mentioned that."

"It's not going to be nice for anybody."

"Stay here, make tea, read, do whatever. We'll talk when I get back with Ox." Gideon stepped off the porch and got into his car. He sat for a moment and held his shaking hand in front of his body. It slowly stopped shaking and he started his vehicle and pulled out of his drive.

*

Gideon hadn't been to the airport before and it took him a few minutes to find a parking space that wasn't in the next area code. He carefully made his way to the automatic doors and stepped into the crowded area of fliers and the people that were there to pick them up. He had to suppress a moment of panic and fear before taking a step around the press of people around him. How can it be so crowded, Gideon wondered, the town's not that big! The Waterloo airport wasn't international but it was the only domestic airport that could handle large jets. Gideon made his way to the arrivals board and easily peered over the heads of the people in front of him.

He looked up at the big board and noticed that Jim's plane had already landed, looking over the sea of people that were milling around a coffee counter he smiled. Head and shoulders above everyone else and sporting a huge black beard and shoulder length black hair was the man he called Ox. Jim had been born and raised in a small Northern Quebec logging town and had joined the military as a way to get out of that small town. Gideon found it amusing that the proud French Canadian was now raising sheep in a small Northern Quebec town not three hours from where he was born.

Jim grinned back and strode toward him, dropping a huge olive drab duffle bag onto the floor, ignoring the angry glances of the people that now had to dodge it. The man Gideon called 'Ox' leaned down to crush him in a bear hug, lifting him 6 inches off the ground.

"Good to see you, Cap," Jim said, setting Gideon back on solid ground, his thick Quebec accent still held in place despite years of working in English.

"Good to see you too." Gideon smiled rubbing his side. "Though my ribs would have been happy with a handshake."

Jim shouldered the duffle again, and started following Gideon out of the airport. "Just figured you could use some love after what I read in the paper

33

a few minutes ago. We got in early and I picked up a copy of the local paper and a coffee while I waited."

Gideon grunted.

"Did you confirm anything?" Ox asked.

"That's about the dumbest thing I've ever heard you say." Gideon stopped and turned to face Jim.

The big man held up one hand. "Just checking, Cap. You always told us to check everything."

Gideon grunted and turned back towards the parking lot. "Now you decide to listen to me," he muttered.

"Sorry to hit a sore spot." Jim said softly.

"Nah," Gideon sighed. "What's worse is that guy Jerry Price made me out to be some kind of hero. I can't even be mad at him. I'd like to know where he got his intel, though. My understanding was that our files were pretty much buried with the Kennedy assassination, and Area 51."

"We could ask him." Jim dropped his duffle into the open trunk of Gideon's car.

Gideon narrowed his eyes at him.

"Nicely!" Jim said quickly. "Until it was time to ask, not nicely." He added softly.

Gideon shook his head. "I don't want to do that stuff anymore."

"Then why in the world are you teaching survival techniques to a bunch of Jesus Freaks?" Jim asked as he shoved his huge bulk into Gideon's car.

"It's useful skills, and don't call us Jesus Freaks," Gideon replied. "How to survive in the wild, that kind of stuff. We're not going to be teaching them how to assault a fortified position. Think of it as penance."

Jim frowned and looked out the window, as Gideon pulled out of the parking lot. "Well, Lord knows we could use that."

A long moment passed before Jim turned to Gideon. "You still have the dreams?"

Gideon nodded silently.

Jim looked back out the window. He reached out and tilted the side mirror so he could see behind them.

"This is supposed to be fun, Ox," Gideon said, softly, "we're the last of the original six. It was supposed to be like a reunion."

"It is," Jim said, watching the side mirror. "I just think it's important to talk about the past when we have people we can talk about it with."

Gideon nodded. "Fair enough, there isn't enough of us left to really have a group therapy session."

"We did what we had to do, Cap. It may not have been right, or it may not have been fair, but we did what we had to do," Jim said.

"Keep telling yourself that, Ox. There's always a choice."

"That's what keeps me going, Cap," Jim said, staring at the side mirror. "How's God doing on making the dreams go away?"

"They're not as bad," Gideon snapped. "I get my strength from Jesus to deal with them. I don't just tell myself I didn't have a choice. There's always a choice."

Gideon smiled and looked at Jim. "For example I haven't killed you yet."

Jim laughed and turned to look behind them. "Do you know we're being followed?"

"Yep," Gideon said.

"Do you know who they are?"

"Nope."

"Do you know what they want?"

"Nope."

"Do you know anything about them?"

"They're not circus performers."

"Well that's useful," Jim replied, dryly.

"Could be, can you imagine being attacked by circus performers, all those little guys in white and red greasepaint?" Gideon shivered. "Anyways, there are four of them. Two in the front, two in the back. They've stayed at least two cars behind us the whole way, they've changed lanes and drifted up and down to make it look like they're not interested. They're not bad really."

"Pros?" Jim asked.

"Maybe."

"You know? You're just a fount of information."

"They just peeled off." Gideon said quickly as he watched the car suddenly turn right onto a side street.

"They lost interest?"

"Maybe they just found out what they wanted to know," Gideon replied.

THREE

Gideon set the coffee on the table beside Jim's arm and sat down beside him on the couch. Chris was sitting in the big plush armchair across from them sipping at a steaming cup of tea, staring at Jim.

"Chris, it's impolite to stare," Gideon said.

Chris shook his head. "Sorry.", he said to Jim.

Jim shrugged his big shoulders. "You kinda get used to it."

Gideon leaned back. "So, we had to talk."

Chris sipped his tea and narrowed his eyes on Gideon. "There are questions about whether you should be allowed to do anything at all for the church."

Gideon nodded. "I expected that."

"You did?" Chris asked, surprised.

"It was the natural move after the article hit the paper," Gideon said. "The church has always been worried about its image, and when the question of my, let's say suitability, to lead in any fashion came into question, it's only a short step to denying my service entirely."

"So how can we change that?" Jim asked.

"Honesty," Gideon said.

"You can't," Jim replied. "There's that whole classified thing hanging over our heads."

"Then they'll have to make due with partial honesty," Gideon replied.

"They won't like that," Chris said.

"They can deal with it," Gideon replied, sternly. "I'm not going to let them judge my past and then say they won't allow me to serve their kids."

"Look at the Captain." Jim muttered. "Getting all worked up about teaching kids to make fire!"

Gideon shook his head. "It's about more than that, Ox." Gideon paused, trying to make sense of the thought growing in his head. "It's about ensuring that our youth are going to be valuable contributions to the future. It's about making sure that they make the right choices now so that maybe, sometime in the future, there won't be a need for people like we were."

Jim smiled and stared at something that neither Gideon nor Chris could see. "That'd be nice, Cap." Then he shook his head and seemed to come back to the present. "But for right now, this situation seems to hinge on these people believing that you can teach their kids safely."

"Right now the question is more, are their kids safe being taught by him," Chris said.

"What's the difference?" Jim asked.

"In one case the kid is hurt because something goes wrong due to Gideon's negligence. In the other case Gideon causes the injury willfully," Chris said.

"I'd wash my hands of the whole thing, Cap." Jim said, throwing his hands in the air. "These people call themselves Christians? What happened to forgiveness? What happened to love? We were talking about choices on the way here, remember, well it looks like they've made a choice."

Gideon nodded. "I understand what you're saying, Ox. In this situation the forgiveness and love has to come from me."

Jim shook his head. "I don't get this." He took a long sip of his coffee. "Those kids will be the safest they've ever been hanging around with you."

"That's not what the parents are seeing right now. What they're seeing is a man that has killed, that has taken another life. A man that has lived a violent and sin filled life that goes against everything that Christianity teaches. It also goes against the basic beliefs of the Church of God, one of the most important is pacifism," Chris said. "And now he wants to teach their kids. It doesn't matter what he wants to teach them, just that he wants to teach them."

"So what are you going to do, Cap?" Jim asked. "What are you going to say?"

"I already told you," Gideon replied. "I'm going to answer all their questions as truthfully as I can, given the law. Then when all that's done, I'm going to tell them what's going to happen."

Chris narrowed his eyes at Gideon. "What's that supposed to mean?"

Ox laughed. "It means he's already figured the outcome of the meeting and he's not going to worry about it."

*

A few hours later, Chris had gone home, and Jim had been shown to the guest room where he was taking a nap. Gideon was standing at the front window, staring out at the street, taking deep breaths, in through the nose, out through the mouth. He turned and stepped back to the couch, where he picked up his Bible. Just as he was opening it to 2 Corinthians, the phone rang. Gideon lifted it and said hello.

"Mr. Steele?" the voice on the other end said. "This is Jerry Price, we spoke briefly the other day."

Gideon immediately wanted to slam the phone down and change his number, but something deep inside him whispered to him to keep talking to this man. "What can I help you with?" he said, cautiously. "I still can't comment on anything from my military days."

"I know you won't tell me anything about your time with the military, sir," Price said. "I just wanted to ask you some questions about how your life is different now."

"How do you mean?" Gideon asked.

"I mean, what's different now?" Price clarified. "You used to be a soldier. Now you're a part of a church and taking kids out on camping trips."

"I'm sure that there are a lot of former military personnel that do the same things."

"I'm sure there are, sir, but not any of them have the focused training that you did." Price quipped.

Gideon made a clicking sound with his tongue.

"Are you denying the training files I have?" Price asked.

"I'm not being drawn into a conversation about it, that's for sure." Gideon said, with a laugh.

"I'd love to meet with you so we can talk about your involvement with the camping trip."

Gideon's eyes went wide as an idea came to him. "Do you know where the Forest Hills Church of God is?"

"That's the church you go to, right?"

"Yes, that's it. Be there tonight at seven," Gideon said, with a smile. "You'll see exactly how my life is different now."

*

Gideon walked into the basement meeting room of the church with the grace and dignity of the former military officer that he was. He had thought, briefly, about wearing his uniform, but dismissed it when Jim had said that it would just draw their attention away from who he was then versus whom he had become. Jim walked beside and just behind him, an imposing force that seemed to hover around Gideon. They both took seats near the back of the room and waited. Gideon was far from feeling the grace and dignity that he showed. His stomach was succumbing to the ache that seemed to have been present since the article first ran. He closed his eyes and murmured a short prayer for strength and courage. He looked around for a moment for Jerry Price, then realized he had no idea what the man looked like. He smiled, half expecting a man in a fedora with a slip of paper in the band that read 'PRESS'.

Some of the parents were openly staring at Gideon with disgust and anger in their eyes, others looked at him and his even bigger friend with awe. There were also a few that looked with pity, those few that called themselves Gideon's friends that were there to do their part to try to help him.

Gideon ignored them all, once in a while leaning over to Jim and saying something in his ear that would make the big man smile, once even belting a laugh out loud. Gideon realized that he had fallen into the same type of coping mechanism that he had when he was in combat. Humour and joking masked the fear and nervousness in his body. He wondered if it meant that he was falling into the same mindset he had back then as well, but then dismissed that idea. Jesus is my Lord now, not war, he assured himself.

John Rogers stepped up to the podium at the front of the room and shuffled a few papers around. He pulled a pair of reading glasses from the top of his head and perched them on his nose.

Jim leaned over. "He has notes for this? I thought it was supposed to be informal, just questions and answers."

Gideon shrugged. "He's probably the most organized man I've ever met. He has lists for everything. He'd have done well in Intelligence."

"Couldn't have done worse." Jim grumbled bringing a smile to Gideon's face. "Kinda reminds me a bit of that intel officer we met in Somalia."

John cleared his throat and the room started to quiet down. "Good evening everybody. We're here to just bring up some concerns that have arisen due to an article in the newspaper regarding Gideon Steele, whom is slated to be our survival expert for the upcoming youth survival week camping trip."

A middle aged lady stood and held her hand up.

"Just a moment, Karen, and we'll open the floor to questions," John said. "I'd like to introduce to you, first, the Camp Committee that is responsible for the programming and running of the youth camp. Pastor Chris Taylor is the chair and pastoral representative," Chris stood and nodded at John. "Sara Michaels is the vice-chair and the Board of Directors representative for the committee," Sara stood and gave a brief wave of her hand, looking around and then smiling warmly at Gideon. "The two other voting members are Craig Morris, and Rachael Davis." The two people stood and then sat down again quickly. "Now I believe I'll introduce to those of you that have never met him, Gideon Steele."

Gideon stood and started to walk towards the podium. John held up his hand and said, "If it's okay with you, Gideon, we'll field questions for the camp committee first."

Gideon nodded and sat back down beside Jim, who leaned over to whisper, "Don't screw up the lists." Gideon grinned.

John ticked something on the podium with his finger and then looked up. "Are there any questions for the camp committee?"

The middle aged woman named Karen stood immediately. "I would like to know how it came about that a murderer came to be in charge of a planned trip with a group of teenagers in the middle of a forest?"

Chris stood up and strode to the podium. "I think we should refrain from using terms like 'killer' when we're talking about Mr. Steele," he said. "I can assure you that he is a firm man-of-God and he has many things to teach the youth of the Church of God."

"But he has killed," Karen said. "I'm not sure that a man that has it within himself to kill should be teaching the youth."

"We're not here to judge his past, Karen, the apostle Paul had also killed." Chris said. "And just like Paul, that was the man that he was before he came to Christ."

"And you're asking us to place the safety and care of our youth in the hands of a man that has killed only God knows how many people!" Karen went on, ignoring Chris' statement. A few of the other parents now were nodding. "A man that had dedicated his life to violence and now we are to believe that he's changed just in a few short years?"

"Karen. . ." Chris started to say.

Gideon took a deep breath. This is the moment, he felt within his chest.

41

He stood, straightened his back and started walking.

"No," Karen said flatly. "These are our children that we're talking about here. We have a responsibility to . . ."

Karen stopped talking when she saw Gideon moving slowly and purposefully to the front of the room, heading directly for the podium. He smiled warmly at Chris and nodded. "I'll take it from here," he said flatly.

He turned to face the room and looked out over the people. He saw a mixture of emotions, from anger all the way to pity, but he wasn't even sure why the pity was there. He realized with a shock that he might even feel the same way that they did if he were in their shoes. He forced himself to stand tall, with his back straight, head up. His stomach was rolling, and his heart pounded against the inside of his chest. Blood was throbbing through his temples and he could hear the rush in his eardrums with each beat of his heart.

His eyes found Karen and he held her gaze. There was anger in her eyes, Gideon was all too familiar with that look. "Ask me the question you want to ask," he said flatly to her. He forced himself to hold her angry gaze with compassion and peace in his. Bile rose for a moment in his throat and he forced it down.

Karen swallowed and some of the anger drained from her face. She had a hard time holding Gideon's eyes. They were blue, and calm. Not at all what she was expecting the eyes of a killer to be. She swallowed again.

"Is it true?" she asked softly.

"Is what true?" Gideon asked, holding her gaze with his calm, blue eyes.

"What the paper wrote about." Karen said standing up a little more. "What it wrote about you."

"Most of what I did was classified and I'm not allowed to talk about it," Gideon started. "I can tell you that yes, I have killed people. I've killed many people." The last part he said plainly, like he was talking about the weather. The calmness in his voice surprised him and he waited a beat before continuing. "I am a different man now, though. I originally started coming to this very church because I was looking for some way to atone for the lives that I've taken and the many more lives that I've ruined, the children, or the wives of the men I killed."

Gideon looked up at the ceiling for a moment and smiled. "I actually

42

thought that I could atone for my sins by going to church and praying, and giving my tithe, maybe help out by setting up and putting away chairs for the pot-luck lunches." He looked down at the people in front of him again. Karen had sat down and was listening to him intently but her face was still stony. "I was wrong. I couldn't make up for the lives I took. All I could do was make my life better."

Jim leaned forward in his seat and cocked his head to one side. Gideon smiled. It was a gesture he was used to, it meant he was carefully evaluating and soaking in every word.

"So I tried. I tried to live my life like the Bible told me to live my life. I found that it was impossible to do without the help of Jesus. So I made the leap of faith. I've jumped out of planes at 35,000 feet, I've been trained to be independent and to make quick decisions and adapt and improvise when things go wrong. Trusting Jesus was the hardest thing I have ever done in my life. Surrendering control to Him and allowing Him to work through me, that was almost impossible for me."

Gideon laughed ruefully and shook his head, "I wish I could explain to you what it's like to have done so many terrible things and then have someone tell you, 'You are forgiven.' It's too much of a gift to accept. It's like I was expecting some kind of horrible thing to come down and force me to pay for my sins and then I'd be forgiven. I practically wanted it!

"I was diagnosed with PTSD after my last mission. I still have the nightmares and some days I'm just holding on by a thread to face the panic and fear, but I am holding on, because Jesus forgave me. Some days I think that's the price that I pay for my forgiveness, but Jesus doesn't work that way. He is grace personified. He paid my debt and now I stand before you clean and pure, because He forgave me."

Gideon leveled his gaze on Karen again. "And if you don't like it, that's fine, but know this, I will never stop trying to serve God."

Silence had settled through the room and Gideon absently noticed that Jim had leaned back and was nodding at him. He chuckled momentarily. "You know what's ironic about this whole thing?

"I fought, and bled, and killed and watched my friends die so that you could have the freedom to judge me, and deny my right to serve your kids, because I'd done those things."

He shook his head, "Kinda makes you wonder."

43

Gideon turned and started to walk away from the podium.

Sara Michaels stood and held her hand up. "One last question, please." Gideon turned to her and smiled. "What would you be in charge of teaching the youth at the camp?"

Gideon looked thoughtful for a moment. "Basic wilderness survival. How to build a shelter, start a fire. How to catch fish, and how to prepare and cook it. What plants are good to eat and which ones should be avoided. How to navigate by the stars and how to climb a cliff face to get a better view of your surroundings."

"And what, exactly would that teach them?" Karen asked. She seemed genuinely curious.

"Self-confidence. Independence. I can guarantee you a couple things. First, it will be difficult, but not impossible. And second, I will push your kids, and they'll come out of it stronger, braver and more reliable than you could ever imagine."

Sara sat down with a smile on her face. "Thank you, Mr. Steele."

Gideon continued on to his seat and sat beside Jim once more. Jim leaned over and nudged his shoulder.

"Hey," he whispered. "Didn't know you could speak so well."

Gideon looked up at the big man, surprised. "You've heard me give hundreds of mission briefings in front of people."

Jim grinned. "Yeah, but this time I believed you."

Gideon rolled his eyes as John Rogers took the podium again and seemed to check off another item on the sheet of paper he carried.

"We would like to thank you all for coming out tonight. I know that some of you drove a fair distance to be here, and I know you'd like to get home as soon as possible. Before we adjourn are there any other questions regarding this topic?"

Karen put up her hand again. "I'd like to know when the committee will come to a decision regarding Mr. Steele's participation."

Chris stood and said, "The committee is planning on meeting this Saturday. A final decision will be made then."

Karen nodded. "Thank you."

A couple other questions rang out, how much it would cost and what sort of things the youth would be allowed to bring. Chris fielded most of them, saying that a price had not been agreed upon yet, but that the Church of God in Canada would buy the equipment needed and that the youth would just have to bring clothes. No cell phones, or electronic equipment would be allowed except for emergency electronics, which would be carried by Gideon. Some of the parents laughed at that saying the youth wouldn't like that rule much. Chris countered saying that the point of the trip was to get closer to God.

When the meeting broke up Karen glanced back at Gideon and seemed to examine him for a short while until he looked directly at her, then she turned away, suddenly.

Jim leaned over again. "She's not quite sure what to make of you now."

"I'm not quite sure what to make of me some days," Gideon said, plainly.

"I hear you, Cap." Jim replied.

John Rogers dismissed the meeting and people started to slowly make their way out to the parking lot. John came back to where Gideon and Ox were sitting together quietly waiting for the room to clear.

"You spoke well." John remarked as he turned a chair around to face the two big men. He held a hand out to Jim. "John Rogers." He said by way of introduction.

"Jim Barris. But everyone just calls me Ox." Jim replied in his lilting French accent.

John smiled. "You're a friend of Gideon's?"

"Like a brother." Gideon replied.

John smiled. "It's good to have friends like that. Do you go to a Church of God? There are a couple in Quebec."

"I was raised Catholic," Jim said. "Now I'm just trying to figure out what comes next."

John nodded. "I was raised Catholic too." He paused a beat and then smiled. "So tell me, what comes next?"

Jim grinned back. "I help my friend train some people how to live in a forest."

John stared thoughtfully at Jim's face and then abruptly stood and turned to Gideon. "I'll call you on Saturday night."

He held out his hand and Gideon gripped it warmly. "Thank you, John." Gideon smiled.

"No, Gideon. Thank you, some people needed to hear the things you said today. I was one of them. I need to go speak with Jerry Price now. He introduced himself to me before the meeting." John stood and smiled down at Gideon and nodded at Jim before turning to a man in a plain white dress shirt and jeans standing by the podium carrying a notebook.

*

On the way back to Gideon's house Jim stared out the window at the buildings flashing by. His mind wandering to places that he hadn't thought about in years.

"Gideon, do you really think there's such a thing as redemption?" Jim asked softly.

"I have to, Ox." Gideon replied. "The Bible says I'm forgiven, therefore there is redemption. Jesus already paid the price for our forgiveness. All we have to do is take it."

"Easier said than done, I think." Jim muttered.

"Yes it is."

"Then why bother? Why don't we just go on with our lives and live it the best we can?" Jim asked. "I mean why make it so hard? We have to love everyone, and forgive everyone. That's impossible!"

"Yes it is," Gideon replied. "But while we try to live our lives the way that God wants us to live, we may just be able to make the world a better place, also we need to place our faith, and hope in Jesus Christ to give us the strength to get a little bit closer to what He has planned for us."

"I thought that's what we were trying to do with the military. Make the world a better place, I mean. We were keeping the peace, most of the time."

"And how'd that work out for you?" Gideon said, dryly. "We were peacekeepers, now I'm trying to be a peacemaker."

"What's the difference?"

"A peacekeeper maintains peace with the threat of violence." Gideon said. "A peacemaker creates peace despite the threat of violence. That's what a soldier of God does."

Jim nodded. "So, let's assume that I give my life to Jesus, put my faith in Him, whatever," Jim said. "What's the plan? What's He got in store for me? I get to trade in my peacekeeper hat for a peacemaker hat? I join you in becoming a solder of God?"

"How am I supposed to know?" Gideon said, shrugging his shoulders. "All I know is that I'm forgiven, and for me, that's a step closer to redemption

46

and peace."

Gideon glanced in his rear view mirror and saw the same car that had followed them from the airport behind them again. There were only two men in the car this time, wearing the same clothes as earlier that day.

"You seeing this?" Gideon muttered.

"Yeah, they've been following us for a while," Jim said.

"And you didn't think it was pertinent information?"

"Well we were talking about forgiveness and redemption and all that stuff." Jim pleaded.

Gideon nodded. "We need to find out who these guys are."

Jim looked around and noticed the alleys that spread from the road at the middle of each block. "Remember the security guys that were following us in Tehran?" he said, with a grin.

Gideon nodded and laughed. Suddenly he pulled the car violently to the right and down one of the alleys. He slammed on the brakes and Jim leapt out of the car and ducked behind a dumpster.

With his foot slamming back down onto the gas, Gideon's car lurched ahead again and approached the end of the alley.

The car that was tailing them spun into the alley, tires squealing and saw Gideon's car pull out onto the road and turn left. He moved cautiously forward and approached the exit.

Suddenly, Gideon's car flew back into the alley in reverse, forcing the trailing car to slam it into reverse and pull back. Right into the dumpster that Jim had pulled out into the middle of the alley.

Jim crept up along the side of the car and positioned himself behind the passenger door.

Gideon opened his door and ducked behind it, peeking around the door for weapons.

The driver's side window slowly slid down and a hand came out holding an ID badge in a black leather holder.

"CISD." A voice from inside the car called.

"Canadian Industrial Security Directorate?" Jim stood and looked into the passenger window where the man in the passenger seat was holding up his ID as well. The Canadian Industrial Security Directorate is responsible for all the security measures put on any information or intelligence gathered by any means for Canada. They are also responsible for the leading an investigation of any breaches of those security measures along with the Royal Canadian Mounted Police.

Gideon stood and walked over to the open window and plucked the ID from the man's hand. "Looks real, Ox."

Jim walked from the back of the car to join Gideon at the driver's window. "Nice to meet you, sorry about the bumper," He said, with a smile.

"Greg Evens." The dark skinned man in the driver's seat said, holding his hand out for the ID, which Gideon handed to him.

"Well, Mr. Evens, could you please explain why you were tailing us?" Gideon asked, leaning down into the car to look at the other man in the car.

In the passenger seat sat a man about 40 years old and sporting a moustache that made him look even more like a federal agent. Both men were wearing jeans and button down shirts.

"We're just trying to keep an eye on you, given that there was obviously a breach in the security measures on your file," Evens said, casually.

"You're thinking that I'm involved in that?" Gideon asked.

"Were you?"

"I don't think I was." Gideon looked up at Jim. "Were you?" he asked with a smile.

Jim laughed shortly. "No I'm pretty sure I wasn't." He said, slowly he leaned closer to Evens. "Were you?"

"You guys can joke all you want but there are some pretty cheesed off people in Ottawa right now," Evans said. "One of them is your former boss, the Minister of Defense."

"Take a look at the people in Ottawa," Gideon said. "Or ask Jerry Price, he's the one that wrote the article."

Evens nodded. "We did, he's telling us he didn't get a name. We already carried out a warrant to get the copies of the files back. Not that it does any good now that the article went to print," He said, frankly.

"So much for intelligence security." Jim muttered. Evens glared at him.

"Hold up, so you're telling me that you have no leads at all? I thought all those files had to be signed out whenever someone wants to see them." Gideon held his hands between Jim and Evens.

Evens looked back at Gideon. "They do. But no one's signed them out since you retired."

Gideon looked down and pinched his lower lip between thumb and index finger. Jim had seen the action hundreds of times when he was thinking and gave him a minute before slapping him softly in the shoulder.

"What are you thinking?"

"The leak, I'm wondering why the leak made my file public." Gideon said, then he looked up at Evens. "Who called you in?"

"Some Special Operations guy, Colonel Matthew Yim." Evens replied.

"He was our CO back in the day." Jim said. "Tell him we said 'hi'."

Gideon nodded. "We need to find out the source for the article."

Evens shook his head. "We tried that, were you listening to me? Price won't give up his source. Says it was an unnamed contact. Besides, we're here to investigate it, not you. We don't need any ex-super soldier cowboy stuff from you."

"Let me talk to him," Gideon said. "Besides if you're tailing ability is any indication you could use the help."

"We're investigators, not spies." Evens said. "Stay out of it, I mean it. I've got the actual authority to arrest people, you guys are just private citizens now, remember that, no Rambo crap."

Gideon nodded his thanks and took the business card that Evens offered him.

"Got it," Jim said with a smile. "No Rambo crap, sir!" He snapped a crisp salute.

"Give me a call if you're in trouble," Evens said, with a smile. "I won't be far away."

Tucking the card in his pants pocket Gideon headed back to his car without a word. When Jim got into the passenger side Gideon turned to face him.

"Something bother you about that?" Gideon muttered.

"You mean besides the whole, 'government agency following us because a top secret file went public' thing?" Jim said, dryly. "And if those guys were military, I'm a midget."

"Why would Yim be interested in a classified file that went public? Sure I served with him, but if he's a spec-ops Colonel now, he's got bigger fish to fry." Gideon said, ignoring Jim. "What does he care? The Commanding Officer of Special Records should have notified them, not Stone." He turned to face Jim. "No one in CISD is military, they're all civilian. It's to preserve objectivity in the investigations."

"Maybe Yim just wanted to make sure it was reported properly." Jim offered. "Like you said, he did serve with you."

Gideon shook his head. "He hated my guts, 'cause I would challenge him on operational tactics."

Jim frowned. "Did you notice they never actually told us why they were following us? They just kinda skimmed over it, like it was SOP." Standard Operational Tactics. "Something stinks about this whole thing, Cap."

"We'll go see Price in the morning. Hopefully he'll have something more than that."

"And here I thought we weren't gonna do any Rambo crap." Jim nodded. "I wonder what my second day in Forest Hills will be like."

FOUR

Kyle Borden was red faced and fuming when Jerry Price walked into his office at 9:03AM. Jerry had arrived at his desk a minute before and was told that Kyle was looking for him. With a confused shrug he turned toward his editor's office.

"You wanted to see me?" he said, as he walked into the office and closed the door.

"Some government agency was in here last night and ripped up our filing room looking for those documents you brought in!" Kyle bellowed. "Did you steal them? I thought you said your contact gave them too you!"

Jerry spread his hands out, palms up. "He did. He told me he had copies made." he offered. "I did everything properly and by the book."

"Well the guys that were in here last night say that whoever gave you those files had no authorization to have them at all! That would make you an accessory after the fact to trafficking National Security Secrets!" Kyle's face was getting redder as he spoke.

"Wait a minute, I don't know who got those files from wherever they got them." Jerry said, quickly, trying to calm Kyle. "Let that guy burn, whoever he is."

Kyle shook his head but it seemed to Jerry like it was waving in a strong breeze. "What you do now is keep your nose clean! You ... cooperate with ..."

Jerry stood. "Kyle calm down, please."

"whatever they ... ask of ... you ... until," Kyle fell over in his chair and slumped to the ground, clutching his chest. "Can't ... breathe."

Jerry jumped to his side.

"Help!"

*

Gideon pulled the car into a parking spot at the offices of the Forest Glen Star and jammed it into park. He turned to face Jim, "You didn't have to come."

51

Jim shrugged. "What was I gonna do? You don't have a T.V. and all you have to read are books about the Bible."

"Could have read one of those," Gideon said, as he got out of the car. "You were saying you wanted redemption."

"I want redemption and peace, not a PhD in Theology." Jim shut his door and the two men started walking towards the double-glass doors. "Big building," Jim shielded his eyes against the sun, and looked up at the fifth floor windows. "For such a small town," he added.

"The presses are all here as well. The only offices are on the fourth floor. It is just a small town."

The two men wove their way through the lobby and towards the elevators. Crowding in with a couple other people Gideon hit the button for the fourth floor. One middle aged man in a shirt and tie looked him up and down and then started.

"Are you Gideon Steele?" he asked, "I saw your picture in the paper."

Gideon nodded. "Yes, sir, I am." He kept his eyes straight, staring at the numbers. "Just going to go and chat with Mr. Price."

The man gulped and turned his eyes forward.

Jim leaned down to Gideon's ear. "That was mean."

Gideon smiled. "A little fun, though."

When the doors opened to the fourth floor Gideon and Jim stepped out and looked both ways.

"Help!" Came a cry from up the hall.

Gideon pushed his way through the people, heading towards the cries for help. A large crowd was gathered around a door.

"Everyone always wants a look, eh Cap?" Jim shouldered his way through, making a space for Gideon. Jerry had taken his tie off and unbuttoned the top two buttons of Kyle's shirt.

"Someone's already called 911, but I think he's not breathing," Jerry said, after a moment of shock at seeing Gideon.

Gideon stood for a moment taking in the sight. An older man lying on the floor, skin deathly pale, Jerry Price, the man that wrote the article, with his panic stricken face kneeling beside the downed man. Gideon's mind raced, his heart pounded in his chest, everything sped up, and turned a strange black and white, like old, grainy film. What happens next? What happens next? Gideon was starting to pant, his hands opening and closing as he tried to get a clear picture of what. . .

"Cap?" Jim suddenly clapped a big hand on Gideon's shoulder. "You alright?"

Gideon nodded and dropped to his knees beside the man that he assumed was Kyle Borden, Jerry's editor. The name plate that once sat on the desk was now sitting on it's edge by the struggling man's legs.

"Ox, air," Gideon said, tersely. The panic started rising again in his chest but he pushed it down, focusing on the man lying in front of him.

"On it." Jim pushed Jerry back and straightened Kyle's airway, leaning his ear down to his mouth. "No breath sounds. Starting AR"

Gideon felt at Kyle's wrist, just below the thumb for a pulse and shook his head. "No pulse. Starting compressions." Leaning over Kyle's chest Gideon locked his fingers together, then straightened his elbows and started pushing down onto Kyle's chest with his upper body weight.

After a few compressions a crack erupted from Kyle's chest. "That's gonna hurt later." Gideon muttered.

"Let's just keep him alive for now," Jim commented between breaths. "We can worry about saying sorry later."

Gideon turned his head and saw a young woman standing with her hand on her mouth. "You!" he said, looking right at the woman. "Go downstairs and wait for the paramedics. Tell them he has no pulse or beath sounds and we've started CPR and to get up here ASAP!"

The woman rushed out of the office.

When the paramedics arrived Gideon leaned back and stood slowly. "One of his ribs broke and I felt another crack as I was doing compressions," he said, stretching his back.

The paramedic nodded. "How long were you at it?"

"About 5 minutes." Gideon replied.

The paramedics quickly checked for a pulse and breathing, nodding to themselves they strapped a oxygen mask over Kyle's head and a blood pressure cuff around his arm.

"His heart is beating again and he's breathing now." One paramedic said as they lifted Kyle onto the stretcher. "Good work." They then rushed the gurney down the hall and into the waiting elevator.

At Jim's insistence people began slowly wandering back to their desks, leaving Gideon, Jim and Jerry Price alone in the office.

Jerry's hands were shaking and he slumped down into the chair he was sitting in before Kyle collapsed. He passed a hand over his face and then seemed to suddenly realize he wasn't alone. He looked at Gideon and then at Jim.

"Thank you, both," Jerry said.

Jim smiled. "Is Forest Hills always so interesting?"

Gideon sat down in a chair opposite Jerry's, his hands clasped in front of him to hide their shaking. "Don't mind him, he just got in from Quebec." He quipped, his heart not really into it.

Jerry smiled wearily. "I remember seeing him last night."

"Did I answer some of your questions you had for me?"

"Yes you did." Jerry nodded. "I'm sure you didn't just come up here to ask me that question. What do you want?" His reporter's mind was racing with possibilities.

"I need the name of your contact." Gideon locked his eyes on Jerry's.

Jerry shook his head. "CISD already asked that. It was an unnamed source."

"Something about this whole thing doesn't make sense. CISD doesn't go around carrying out warrants and questioning people," Gideon said, softly. "They're investigators and database managers, they might ask the occasional question over the phone, but they usually get the Mounties to do the face to face stuff. This is bigger than your story." Gideon turned his head to follow Jerry's as he looked away.

"Your file was missing the After Action Reports," Jerry said, "That's odd isn't it?"

"Yes it is," Gideon said, softly, glancing up at Jim, who was looking a little worried. "Something is going on here that we need to figure out. Right now your boss is fighting for his life, and that should be your priority."

Jerry seemed to struggle for a moment, the reality of the event that had just happened falling on him like a huge weight. Gideon knew that he was close, he had to tread softly here, one wrong push would close Jerry's mouth and the name would be lost forever. So Gideon waited, he watched as Jerry struggled with his conscience and with the events that had just happened. His hands shook and he kept wiping sweat from his brow and wiping it on his pants.

The poor guy's almost ready to snap. Gideon thought.

Jerry's shoulder suddenly sagged and he let his head drop, his chin resting on his chest. A sob erupted from his chest.

Lord, please give him comfort. Gideon prayed silently as he reached out to place his big hand on Jerry's shoulder.

"I can't." Jerry shook his head. "A journalist doesn't give up his sources."

"Journalist." Ox snorted. "How many people does this paper reach, a hundred?"

"HEY!" Jerry shot out of the chair standing face to chest with Ox "If a soldier's unit only has three people, does it make him any less of a soldier?!" Jerry's eyes widened as he realized he was poking Ox in the chest. He backed up slowly, and sat back down.

"Spunky." Ox smiled. "I like him." Gideon smiled and shook his head at the Frenchman.

"I gave my word." Jerry whispered. "What do I have, if not my integrity?"

"God." Gideon answered without hesitation.

"Not sure I could face Him if I broke my word." Jerry closed his eyes. "Look, I'm not giving up my source . . . but I will contact him and try to get him to give himself up."

"That's. . ." Ox started.

"Thank you." Gideon cut him off.

Jerry looked up suddenly. "It's my job to report the truth, and maybe . . . maybe I let the story get to me," he said. "I'm sorry you're going through all this."

Gideon stood, "I forgive you," he said, knowing it was what Jerry needed to hear.

Jim watched on, his head tilted and smiled slightly. When Gideon said the last words he nodded. Something was starting to make sense but it was like a light, just outside of his field of vision. He could make out the glow, but not the exact source of the idea he was trying to grasp at.

Gideon seemed to have his PTSD under control, but every once in a while Jim saw the tremor in his hand or the sudden intake of breath as the stress caught him. Yet here he was, forgiving the source of a lot of that stress. There was something that happened to both of them, like a weight had been lifted from them. Gideon seemed to walk with more confidence as they made their way back to the car.

Jim looked around, more out of habit than anything else and suddenly laughed. Gideon glanced at his friend, confused. Jim pointed across the street.

"They changed cars." He said.

Following Jim's finger, Gideon saw Evens and his partner in a blue Buick Regal sitting quietly watching him. When Jim pointed, Evens hung his head in shame.

"Let's go say hi." Gideon offered and the two men wandered across the street, dodging cars and stood by the driver's window, which Evens lowered.

"Hi, guys," Evens said.

"That's what I was gonna say." Gideon laughed.

Evens and the other agent were wearing the same windbreakers as before with new clothes underneath. Jim shook his head. "Loose the jackets guys, or at least don't wear matching ones. Little tip from surveillance 101, free of charge."

"I told you, we're investigators, not spies. I usually spend my time looking at security video feeds and data mining hard drives." Evans said to Jim.

Jim glanced over to Gideon and mouthed the words, 'data mining' with a confused look. Gideon shrugged his shoulders.

"What happened in there?" Evens asked turning to Gideon and ignoring Jim.

"Guy had a heart attack, Ox and I saved him, then we asked Jerry who his source was." Gideon replied matter-of-factly.

"My second day in Forest Glen is turning out pretty eventful too." Jim said with a smile. "The last time I had this much fun was when a storm knocked down a section of fence in one of my fields. Sheep got out, it was a mess, took me two days to find them all."

"Did you get the name?" Evens asked, smiling at Jim.

"No, you were right he clammed up and said it was an unnamed source," Gideon said. "He did mention that the After Action Reports were missing from my file."

"Yeah they weren't in the files that we picked up with the warrant either," Evens said. "You have any clue where they may be?"

56

Gideon shook his head. "No clue, it's not my problem anyways."

Evens smiled. "So you just gonna go back to retirement?"

"Pretty much, think we'll do some pricing of equipment for the church camping thing, then make sure the guy who had the heart attack is okay after lunch." Gideon replied. "You have any idea where my after action reports went?"

Evens shook his head. "No idea." He started the car. "We're being called back to Ottawa, we've run down everything we can here. No offense, but you're useless to me now."

Jim leaned in through the window and said, "Seriously guys, get a second car and split up, if you ever have to do this again. The two of you in here all the time is a little creepy."

Evens started raising the window on Jim's head with a smile and Jim had to pull back quickly before getting caught in it. He smiled at the CISD agents and wandered back to the car.

"I like those guys." He called with a grin to Gideon.

"You also liked the little reporter who was poking you in the chest." Gideon paused as he opened his door and looked at Jim appraisingly. "Maybe you need to see a therapist."

Jim stuck his tongue out at Gideon before getting in the car.

When they were safely in the car Jim turned to face Gideon, a serious look back on his face. "Okay, spill it why'd you lie to them?"

"I didn't really lie." Gideon replied. "I just didn't tell him that we MAY be able to find out the guy's name."

"Whatever."

"I don't trust them," Gideon said. "We don't know why they're here tailing us. We don't know why they seem to have the authority to carry out warrants, and we don't know why my file was missing the after action reports and they don't seem too worried that part of my file is missing. Keeping secure documents secure is their job. Now one of the most classified files has been leaked, and parts of it are missing and these guys pack up and go home because the lead runs cold? I'd be pretty ticked if we got called out of a mission, just because our next move was blocked."

"Maybe they know where the after action reports are." Jim offered. "Maybe the reports weren't there in the first place and they knew that."

Gideon nodded, placing this puzzle in the back of his mind and pulled out of the parking lot.

*

The rest of the morning Gideon and Jim spent in small wilderness stores and camping outlets, pricing military quality back backs, and sleeping bags. They stopped at one climbing store in Kitchener, a neighboring city, to price ropes and harnesses and the various equipment they'd need for rock climbing.

"John's going to have a heart attack when he sees this bill," Jim said, as he added everything on a notepad he'd picked up at a dollar store along the way.

"He'll blame Chris, Chris'll blame me and I'll blame you," Gideon said.

"Me?"

"Why not? I've blamed stuff on you for years." Gideon pulled into a McDonalds.

Jim looked to the roof of the car. "Mon Dieu!"

After lunch they headed over to St. Mary's Hospital, the only hospital in Forest Glen. Jim remarked absently that every town seemed to have a St. Mary's Hospital. Gideon shrugged and said it must make people feel better, knowing the Mother of Jesus was watching over them.

They headed to information and asked about Kyle Borden saying that he was brought in that morning with a heart attack. When asked if they were family, they said, no, they were the men that performed CPR until the paramedics got there. The nurse smiled at them.

"The Good Samaritans!" she exclaimed. "You probably saved his life. He's been asking about you since we told him what happened."

"He's awake?" Gideon asked, surprised.

"He is," the nurse said. "Won't be running any marathons for a while, but his is awake and responding well to the treatment."

She pointed them down a hall and told them what room Kyle Borden was in.

The door was open and Gideon knocked on the doorframe to announce themselves. Kyle turned from where he was staring out the window and smiled.

"I understand I need to thank you two," he said hoarsely. His skin was grey and almost translucent, an oxygen mask covered half his face and Gideon noticed that he still looked sickly, but had a much better glow about

58

him than the last time he saw the older man. Tubes and wires ran from bags and machines around the bed to monitor every part of his body function and he looked like he was too weak to raise his head, but he pulled an arm from under the sheet and beckoned them forward.

The two big men walked into the room and sat down on plastic chairs. Gideon reached out and took Kyle's hand. "A pleasure to meet you," he said with a smile. "Sorry about the ribs."

Kyle laughed weakly. "The least of my worries," he said. "The doctor tells me my diet, stress and a 50% blockage in one of my arteries is the bigger concern. I'm slated for coronary angioplasty surgery as soon as I'm strong enough. Doc says probably tomorrow, maybe the next."

Jim laughed. "A cakewalk compared to having him bounce on your chest." He tossed a thumb at Gideon.

Kyle looked down at the sheets for a moment. "I wanted to thank you both for saving my life, and to apologize to you, Gideon for what we've put you through."

Gideon shook his head. "Already forgiven."

"Jerry Price sent me his article about the meeting last night. I had no idea our reporting about your training would cause that much turmoil." Kyle added, his face darkening. "I should fire him for being so stupid." Kyle suddenly shook his head, "No, I should resign for being so stupid. Kyle did everything he was supposed to do and I ran the story, I put my seal of approval on it."

Gideon shook his head. "That won't accomplish much."

Jim glanced over at his friend in surprise.

"What do you mean?" Kyle asked.

"I talked to Jerry and I forgave him. We fought," Gideon looked up and smiled at Jim, "so that the press could be free to print the truth, and I'd like to live in a town where the editor makes sure that happens. We talked. I forgave him, it's all finished. Now you and I have talked, and I forgive you." Gideon explained. "There's no need for any firing, or resigning."

Kyle looked thoughtfully out the window again. "My Dad was a Baptist Minister. He always said that people deserved a second chance, and, if needed, a third or fourth." He laughed sadly. "Forgive, forgive, forgive, he'd say. Seventy times seven times. That's somewhere in the Bible."

"Matthew 18:22." Gideon supplied. "A favorite of mine."

59

Jim looked on and could sense that feeling of something happening just outside of his vision again. Some idea he couldn't quite grasp. He pulled out the dollar store notebook and wrote down the scripture, vowing to look it up when he could.

"When my wife passed, I said I was going to start going back to church again. That never happened. Too much to do, too much work. Maybe when I can drive again I'll come out and visit this church of yours."

Gideon shook his head. "Not my church, sir. It's God's. I'll come and drive you the Sunday after you get out."

Kyle nodded, his eyelids starting to droop. "I think I'd like that."

After a moment Kyle was sleeping. Gideon and Jim walked in silence out to the car. When they were both in and Gideon pulled out into traffic Jim turned halfway in his seat to face him.

"You really buy into all this forgiveness and grace stuff don't you?" Jim's tone wasn't angry, more shocked.

Gideon nodded. "Yep."

"Why?"

"I believe it," Gideon said, with a deep breath. "It gives me peace knowing that I'm forgiven for all the things that I've done. Now I try to live with love and forgiveness in me, and I can make others feel that way by forgiving as well, like Jerry Price. Don't get me wrong, it's the hardest thing I've ever had to do, to live like Christ, but it's worth it in the end, because I know that I can be an example to everyone else of what it's like to live like Christ."

"You still hurt, Cap," Jim said. "I see it, your hands shake once in a while, you suck in breath when you feel stressed. I heard you last night during one of the nightmares. You don't have it all together. Maybe that 'forgive others' Bible verse of yours is intended to be read to forgive yourself as well."

Gideon nodded, pushing down a rising panic. "That's true, but I'm happier now than I was when I first got out." Gideon glanced over to Jim and smiled. "And did you miss the part where I said it was hard? It was hard forgiving those guys today, they made my life really uncomfortable lately, but I said the words and I'll follow through, even if it's hard and I don't want to. We've done some pretty hard stuff, you and I, but this makes everything look like a cakewalk compared to it, especially the forgiving yourself part."

"You're not a very good salesman." Jim shook his head.

"I'm not selling. You know as well as I do that most of today I was running on instinct, hardly thinking at all." Gideon turned onto his cul-de-sac. "All I can really tell you is that it's there for you. You just have to have the courage to take it."

*

Gideon had gone upstairs to shower and Jim found himself alone in the living room. He found a Bible and started to flip through it until he found Matthew, then chapter 18 and verse 22.

"Jesus saith unto him, I say not unto thee, Until seven times; but, Until seventy times seven."

Jim furrowed his brow. Seventy times seven was 490. That seemed like a lot of times. Jim read the rest of the passage from verse 21 to 35. The idea just out of his sight started to come in glimpses and flashes, almost, but not quite all there. So Jesus wanted us all to forgive each other, just as He forgave us. Therefore if I forgive, I'll be forgiven. Jim thought. Verse 35 caught his eye.

"So shall also my heavenly Father do unto you, if ye forgive not every one his brother from your hearts."

He was confused about the idea of forgiving from your hearts. What did that mean? He leaned back on the couch and thought some more about it, trying to get a bead on the elusive idea and the fringes of his sight.

*

Gideon was standing under the stream of water from the showerhead and letting it wash away the stress and worries of the day. He was totally unprepared for the pressure of having a man dying on the floor when they got to the newspaper office. He nearly broke down, and might have, if years of training hadn't kicked in. Please, Lord, help me. He silently prayed. In the past 24 hours he had gone from mass murderer at the meeting last night, to hero this afternoon, the switch was too fast and he just wanted to curl up and forget about the world for a few years.

He knew he couldn't. He knew he was flawed, Lord how he knew that, but he also knew that Jesus was on his side, he knew he had the Lord of All on his side and that he would not fail, as long as he stayed on the path that the Lord set before him. Sometimes, however the road was hard to see. Like all the questions surrounding his personnel file. Why was it classified so highly, why were his After Action Reports missing? Why were these CISD agents following him, and what did they want with him? So many questions, not enough answers.

Stepping out of the shower, Gideon dressed and, headed downstairs. He found Jim sitting on the couch reading the Bible that he kept on the end table.

"How's it going?" Gideon asked as he sat down across from him. He sighed and leaned back into the soft chair.

"What's this, forgive from the heart thing?" Jim asked, handing the Bible to Gideon and pointing at the passage.

"Well, it's just like it says." Gideon replied. "I asked Chris the same question and he said that true forgiveness comes from within. Forgiveness that you believe, and not just words that you use to cover something up."

Jim nodded. "And Jesus' forgiveness, that comes from the heart?"

"So says the Pastor, and the Bible."

"I'm gonna have to think about this," Jim said, softly. "It's like something just outside of my sight, and I can't get a good bead on it."

Gideon leaned back and looked out the window. "The search is almost as important as the finding," he said absently.

Gideon threw two frozen pizzas into the oven for dinner and after eating they returned to the living room to read and talk some more. Jim struggled with his thoughts, pouring over passage after passage in the Bible, checking his thoughts against a commentary by his side.

Gideon was struggling his way through a book on Job, when the phone interrupted him.

"Hello?" Gideon said into the handset, glad to put the book down for a few minutes.

"Gideon?" a familiar female voice asked. "It's Sara Michaels."

"Hi, Sara. What can I do for you?"

"I wanted to let you know that I think you'll have no problem with the vote on Saturday. I also wanted to get together for coffee sometime." She paused, then added quickly. "To go over the plans for camp, maybe sometime early next week. If that's good for you?"

"That sounds, great. I'm free anytime." Gideon smiled, Jim looked up from his reading for a moment, a question in his eyes.

"Okay, just let me check my schedule and I'll confirm everything with you on Sunday." Sara replied.

"Sounds good," Gideon said, before he said goodbye and hung up the phone, placing it back on the end table. He picked up the book and started reading again.

Jim set his book in his lap and stared at Gideon, waiting for some kind of reaction.

"Don't," Gideon said, simply without looking up from his book.

Jim played at looking hurt for a moment and then lifted his book again with a smile.

*

The two men were getting ready for bed. Jim was changing in the spare room and Gideon was brushing his teeth in the en-suite next to his master bedroom. Gideon was rinsing his toothbrush and was just reaching for the mouthwash when he heard the knock at his door.

Gideon stepped out into the hall and eyed Jim as he stepped out, his big chest bristling with black hair. Jim shrugged and followed Gideon down the stairs. Gideon opened the front door and saw an athletic man wearing a crumpled blue, suit. His hair was slightly disheveled, his tie was undone and hanging loose around his neck.

"Ummmm, hello?" Gideon said, startled. A cab drove off behind the man on his porch.

"Gideon Steele?" the man asked.

"Yes."

"My name is Kieran James, and I have some questions for you." The man lifted a file folder.

FIVE

Gideon stared at the man in front of him, then he let his eyes drift down to the folder in his hand. It was red with writing along the top cover. The writing said, 'Top Secret'.

"What can I help you with?" Gideon said, cautiously, grabbing the man by the collar and pulling him into the house. He took a quick look up and down the street before closing the door.

Kieran shook his head suddenly, struggling to stand after being pulled in. "I'm sorry. I must look insane. Showing up here late at night, looking like a bum."

"Where did you get that?" Gideon asked pointing at the folder, and locking the door.

Kieran held up the object of Gideon's attention. "This is what I wanted to talk about."

Gideon glanced back at Jim, who was looking over his shoulder at Kieran. His eyes were locked on the folder as well.

"Well come on in," Gideon said, "I'll answer what I can."

Gideon stepped into the living room and closed the curtains tight. Kieran slowly stepped into the room and looked around taking it all in. Jim followed into the living room and leaned against a wall that allowed him a good view of the room and the front door. Gideon sat in the plush chair by the window and, Kieran sat on the couch, facing the window and Gideon.

"Where did you get that file?" Gideon asked again.

Kieran closed his eyes for a moment, and took a deep breath, letting it out slowly. "A friend of mine called asking about you for an article he was writing."

"Jerry Price, yes, we've met." Jim muttered. "You must be his contact."

Kieran nodded and rubbed his tired looking eyes. "Yes, of course. He called me today and asked if I'd talk to you. He said something about CISD being involved. They didn't call me and as far as I know I'm one of the last people to access your digital file. I'd be the first person they'd call!" He paused and sighed. "Anyways, I couldn't find anything about you, nothing at all, except that you were in the military database. No rank, no unit, no nothing!"

He smoothed the file on his legs and stared out through the window into the darkness beyond. "I should have had access to everything, but I was cut out and I couldn't figure out why. So I went to the Governor General, my boss, and asked him about it. When I gave him your name he tapped it into his computer and poof there you were. But something scared him. Something made him nervous. What you need to understand is that I have every shred of access to everything that he does. Yet I couldn't even so much as get your rank."

"So how did you get it?" Gideon asked.

"I bullied some poor Corporal in special records," Kieran said. "But none of your after action reports were where they should have been. That got me to wondering where they were, and why they were missing. So I did a little asking around. I was informed by a very reliable source that the Governor General, the Minister of Defense, and a Special Operations Colonel had a closed door meeting about, of all things, you." Kieran watched Gideon's face carefully, looking for anything. I might as well be watching grass grow, Kieran thought.

Jim stepped forward and leaned down towards Kieran. "And," he asked. "What happened?"

Kieran shook his head. "I don't know. But that evening this file was shoved under my door." He hefted the file up. "This has all of your after action reports and the personnel records of all of the men from your original unit."

It was Gideon's turn to rub his eyes and then run his hands over his bald pate, he was sweating now. "Who gave you that?"

"The same Corporal that found your file." Kieran replied. "He told me to forget his name." he added with a smile.

"Smart kid." Jim muttered. "So why do you want to ask the Captain here questions? It's all in the file isn't it?"

Kieran nodded. "Most of it is. But there are some things that I need to confirm."

"Such as?" Gideon asked, fearing he knew the answer and feeling the tension and pain in his stomach. Father, please be with me. Please forgive me for the things we are about to talk about. Gideon thought.

"What can you tell me about the attack on the Dawson Compound?" Kieran asked.

Jim hissed in a breath through his teeth. Gideon closed his eyes and shook his head. He was sure he was going to vomit.

"Please tell me that what I'm reading between the lines in this report isn't true." Kieran lifted a red page and handed it to Gideon.

He opened his eyes and took the sheet in trembling fingers.

"This operation was doomed from the start." Gideon whispered. He Glanced at it briefly and then handed it back to Kieran. "Forget about it."

"I just want to be clear on who ordered this operation." Kieran pressed as he placed the sheet back in the file. "The RCMP should have handled that. The military shouldn't have been involved even in an advisory role."

"There's always someone who wants to destroy Canada, or America, or some other country." Jim said as he loomed closer over Kieran. "There's always someone who threatens the peaceful little homes that we have here. There's always someone who wants to blow up somebody, or shoot, or burn or hurt someone that's weaker, smaller or just plain different than them. The only thing that stands in their way are the people that do the jobs like we did."

"I'm not here to argue whether or not it was a warranted operation. I want to know who ordered it, and why the military did the job and not the RCMP Special Response Unit." Kieran pressed again.

"It's in the report isn't it?" Gideon asked, knowing full well that it wasn't, he wrote it.

"All it says is that the Minister of Defense ordered the elimination of the Dawson Compound located in Alberta Canada, for crimes against the national security. It doesn't go into any more detail than that." Kieran asked. "If I went to my boss with a report about why we raised the tariff on widgets from Jamaica, and it had a one sentence explanation about why we did it, I'd be fired. Did the Governor General have any input into this operation?"

Jim glanced at Gideon. "Why would he? The Governor General is just a figurehead for the British Crown. He has no actual authority over anything."

"Why would the Governor General have anything to do with an attack on the Dawson Compound?" Gideon asked, staring at the floor, ignoring

67

Jim's probing look. He clasped his hands in front of him to prevent the shaking, and concentrated on his breathing, his chest feeling as firm as a sheet of steel.

"The Dawson Boys were involved in everything from drugs to murder for hire, among those illegal activities was kidnapping, especially high profile targets, like the nephew of a Governor General." Kieran replied. "I did some research about the Dawson's when I read that pathetic excuse for a reason to eliminate 45 people in the compound. The Dawson's kidnapped and tortured Doneven's nephew, the son of his older sister. When she paid the ransom the nephew, a twenty year old in his second year of pre-med, was returned, in four cardboard boxes."

"Ask the Governor General," Gideon said, still not moving his eyes from the cream carpet.

"I have suspicions that if I were to cheese him off by asking these questions, a military special ops team would be looking for me in order to make me disappear." Kieran quipped.

"You're going to need proof if you want to survive this at all," Gideon said. "It won't take them long to find out that you were the one that got the files, and leaked the information."

"That's why I need you." Kieran's eyes pleaded.

"Do you have somewhere to stay?" Gideon asked.

"I'm in a hotel about 5 minutes from here."

Gideon nodded. "I can't help you tonight."

Kieran stood, "Can I meet with you in the morning, then?"

"Come for tea at about ten." Gideon said, standing as well.

Kieran reached into the file and pulled out about 2 dozen 8X10 glossy photos, handing them to Gideon. He looked back at Gideon as he opened the front door. "Just take a look at it and see if I missed anything. Those are photos of the originals. I'm not letting THIS file out of my sight."

"Smart move," Jim said, still keeping half an eye on Gideon. "But you can't go out there waving a red file around. So we've got to hide it." Jim reached over and grabbed the file and turned Kieran around, roughly pulling at the back of his shirt. He slid the file under his pants about halfway and then tucked his shirttail over the visible part above his belt. As a final touch he fluffed the jacket over it all.

"Not perfect, but it'll do." Jim muttered. "Don't let anyone see that file, anywhere at any time."

Gideon nodded at Jim's work. "I doubt you missed anything, and I wrote the report, I know what's in there." Gideon's smile was fake. His breathing was short and clipped now.

Kieran sighed again, his eyes taking in the increasingly haunted look on Gideon's face. "I know a lot of what you did for this country, Gideon, and I know what you've sacrificed." Kieran stared at Gideon's face for a moment. "Will you be alright if I start digging this up?"

"I'll be fine." Gideon said with a certainty he didn't feel. Kieran nodded once and stepped out the door.

"Liar," Jim said as soon as the door closed.

"I will be fine, Ox." Gideon replied. "Right now I'm just tired. Tired of fighting, tired of violence, tired of our past constantly coming back to haunt us. I'm just tired." Gideon lifted his hand over his eyes, and sighed deeply. The first real breath he'd taken since Kieran walked in the door.

Jim placed his hand on his friend's shoulder. "Get some rest, Cap," he said. "Pray, talk to Jesus, whatever it is you do to get that peace you've been telling me about."

"That's the problem isn't it?" Gideon asked softly. When Jim just cocked his head quizzically at him, he went on. "How can I be a peace maker if I don't have peace in my own heart?"

"Let's just make it through this, Cap." Jim said.

Gideon nodded and went up to his room, pausing to pat Jim on the back and mutter goodnight.

Jim stood in the living room and stared at the painting of Jesus on the wall.

"How about just a little help for him, eh?" he said to the painting in French.

*

Gideon seemed fine the next morning. They had slept in until 7AM and when Gideon came downstairs he was smiling, but Jim knew it was fake and forced. Jim hadn't had the nightmares that he was expecting but he had heard Gideon tossing and calling out in his sleep, neither of them made any mention of it.

As Jim prepared the morning coffee, Gideon stood facing the coffee table where the file lay, after a moment he wandered back to the kitchen.

Jim nodded and handed Gideon a mug. Gideon looked at it and frowned.

"What's wrong?" Jim asked.

"I've just gotten used to tea in the morning," Gideon said.

"Sorry," Jim said, with a smile. "I just wanted to be prepared for day number three. Day number two was more interesting than day number one!"

Gideon laughed without humour and took a sip of coffee. "Well we have a busy day today, what with classified documents on my coffee table and all. The camp thing is out of our hands now, just have to wait until they decide what to do with it. They meet tomorrow."

Jim nodded. "I know. I was there, remember?" Jim paused for a breath. "We gonna talk about the Dawson's?"

"Nope," Gideon replied flatly.

Gideon went to the front bay window and pulled back the curtain. Evens car wasn't there, a good sign. Deciding to brave the front porch, he stepped outside and took his customary seat in the wicker chair, his eyes scanning up and down the street.

Jim soon joined him, munching on a piece of toast and setting his coffee on the small table between them. They sat for a long time, just watching the sun slowly shorten the shadows of the front yard as it rose into the sky. Jim watched as his friend seemed to relax more and more with the slow cadence of the rocking chair.

"I could get used to this," Jim said with a grin.

"Don't you just relax back home at all?"

"I herd sheep. Then for a change I shear sheep. Once in a while I sell sheep." Jim shrugged. "That's about it."

"Nothing else?"

"Well," Jim said with a smile. "There was a lady from town. . ."

The two men spent the next two hours talking about their lives, catching up on common people they knew, yet never touching the topic of the friends that they had both lost or the photographs on the coffee table.

"I'm going to Ottawa for a few days," Jim said after a short silence. "I'm going to dig around and see what turns up."

Gideon nodded. "I don't think you'll like what you'll find."

"You 'think' or you 'know'?"

Gideon stared at Mrs. Gable as she pulled her hose out again.

"You've got to talk, man," Jim said, suddenly. "It's going to eat you up inside. I know that you have Jesus and all that, and I'm happy for you, but you need to get this stuff off your chest."

He paused for a moment to take a deep breath. "I looked up 'sin' in one of those Bible books you got. I figured since we've sinned so much I should know what's in store. It led me to James 5:16, 'Therefore, confess your sins to one another, and pray for one another so that you may be healed. The effective prayer of a righteous man can accomplish much.' The first Bible verse I've ever memorized and it's all about us, Cap.

"I may not have been diagnosed with PTSD like you were, but I'm just as messed up. After all we've done to ourselves, don't we deserve a little healing?"

Gideon nodded a fraction of an inch.

Jim stepped into the house and was back out a few moments later in cargo pants with big, bulging pockets in the thighs and a t-shirt. In his hand was the pile of photographs from the table, which he stuffed into one of the big pockets on his thighs.

"I'm going to leave my stuff here if it's okay with you. I want to make a stop back home for a minute anyways, pick up some stuff I'll need." Jim said as he lowered himself back into his chair.

"What's your plan?" Gideon asked, his voice strained.

"I'll drop by to see Yim, I have a feeling he was the Colonel that Kieran talked about last night. Besides something about that whole setup is just wrong. Yim just seems to be in too many places involved in all this."

Gideon nodded. There was a long silence before he spoke again, almost a whisper. "I planned it."

Jim turned his head. "What?"

"I planned the assault on the compound." Gideon stared into his hands, and then he started dry washing them between his knees. "The need to know was so small that I was asked to plan the attack and keep you guys out of operational directives. I was to be the only person that knew the whole plan, you guys were just to know your parts."

"That's normal," Jim said, an unspoken question in his eyes.

"The only other people that knew the whole plan were Yim, and some guy named Patricks."

"Who was Patricks?"

71

Gideon shook his head. "Don't know."

A taxi pulled up and Kieran started to get out of the back seat. Jim stood and told him to wait and hold the cab.

"I'm gonna deal with this, Cap, but you need to talk to Chris or John, hell, even talk to that girl that called you last night, but you aren't going to be worth anything to those kids if you can't keep it together. You're cooped up in this house, you have tea on your porch with a pastor a few times a week and you go to church on Sunday. You put up a good face, but I know you. You're scared of meeting people because you're ashamed of what we've done," Jim said. "I get the shame, Cap, but you need to talk to real people if you want to get over it."

Gideon suddenly stood and grabbed Jim in a hug. "Thanks for coming, Ox, don't be long."

Jim nodded once and headed down the stairs to Kieran who stared at him quizzically.

"You get to spend a few days with me, Shorty," Jim said with a grin. "First I have to stop in Quebec." He slapped the back of his hand into Kieran's chest with a smile and walked to the far side of the cab and got in.

Kieran stood confused and in shock until Jim pounded on the roof of the cab and yelled for him to move. The cab driver turned to tell Jim to be quiet, took a good look at the big man and turned back to the front without saying a word.

Gideon watched in silence as the cab drove away. He took a deep breath and went into the house to wash his dishes. He looked at the coffee table where the file had sat and noticed something else missing. The Bible that he always kept there was gone. Gideon smiled.

*

A few hours later, on a plane headed to Montreal, Jim sat back in his seat. He had briefed Kieran on his plan to try to get some information from his old Commanding Officer, Major, now Colonel, Yim before put the Governor General's Chief of Staff on a flight back to Ottawa. Kieran seemed to like the idea of such a highly placed officer that was still in the Service helping them.

Jim reached into a thigh pocket of his cargo pants and pulled out the worn Bible from Gideon's coffee table, he knew Gideon wouldn't mind him borrowing it, but there was just something about the words in this book that made that glow in the corner of his eyes, almost crystallize into a full idea. He smiled as a steward asked if he wanted a drink, ordered a coffee and leaned back, opening the book.

*

Gideon wandered aimlessly around his house. Moving things that didn't need to be moved, then placing them back. His hands were itchy, his chest tight. He was wearing blue denim jeans and a grey button down shirt that he had tucked into his pants. He checked that the plants in the corner of the living room were straight and then touched the painting of Jesus.

The doorbell almost made him jump, he rushed to the door and opened it.

Sara Michaels stood there smiling. She was wearing a sundress with a light sweater over it.

"Hi," Gideon said.

"Hi," Sara replied.

There was an awkward moment of silence.

"I have tea made if you'd like to sit down." Gideon motioned to the living room.

Sara smiled and sat down on the couch. "I love tea."

Gideon smiled.

EPILOGUE

Gideon woke late the next morning, almost 9 o'clock, which was sleeping in for him. Talking with Sara the night before was therapeutic for him, just as Jim had said it would be. They had talked late into the night, sharing stories of their childhoods, or small tidbits about their likes or dislikes. Eventually the subject found its way to Gideon's military service.

Gideon smiled and took a deep breath before talking about his PTSD, he avoided the details about his service, using broad brush strokes to paint a picture that was violent and frightening. There was a moment of panic that rose in his chest as he thought that he was going to scare her away, but she merely sat there nodding at him to continue, so he did. At one point he had to pause, when talking briefly about some of the friends he had lost. Tears welled in his eyes and he closed them tightly, trying to force them away. Then he felt a small, soft hand in his. Sara was suddenly sitting beside him holding his calloused, worn hand in hers. She looked up into his eyes with compassion, yet not a hint of pity. Gideon wiped the tears from his eyes with the back of his free hand and smiled.

Sara smiled back.

Gideon grinned at the memory as he made his tea. He was startled when the phone rang and picked it up on the fourth ring.

"Hello?" He said, crisply. His smile broadened as he heard Chris' words on the other side of the line.

"The camp is going forward, and you are our survival advisor if you still want to help."

"I do," Gideon replied.

*

Jim stepped out of his hotel room in Ottawa. He wore his dress uniform, ribbons and medals dangled from his chest detailing almost every service he had performed for his country. It had never occurred to him before, but there were a number of missions in a number of countries that he had not received service ribbons for.

He had gone to a small church yesterday morning, the pastor was old, but seemed to really be enthusiastic about what he was speaking on. After, Jim had walked up to the front and spoke for about an hour with the man with the balding head. Jim frowned, he couldn't even remember the pastor's name. When he'd left the church he went straight to a barber shop. Now he sported a close military cut and a fresh shave. A paler area of his tanned skin showed where he had once had his thick, black beard.

Kieran was straightening his tie in front of a mirror across from the hotel room door, waiting to share a cab to the Parliament Buildings.

"Who are you going to see again?" he asked Jim as he turned to face him.

"Colonel Matthew Yim," Jim replied in his lilting Quebecois accent. "He was our old commanding officer, and he was involved with the planning of the mission for the Dawson attack. He might know who this Patricks guy is."

"Can he be trusted?" Kieran asked, tuning to look at Jim.

"Not as far as a three year old could throw him. The Cap and I think he's involved in this somehow." Jim replied without hesitation. "But you can trust me."

"But can I trust you with my life?" Kieran muttered.

Jim frowned and ignored the question, stepping into the elevator and waited for Kieran. He poked the down button with a meaty finger and then casually reached into the right pocket of his dress jacket, gripping Gideon's Bible for a moment.

"I'm a soldier of God, why wouldn't you?" Jim said softly.

*

Evans was sitting at a park bench reading a newspaper article on his smartphone. What a stupid cliché, he thought to himself. Clandestine meeting in a public park, on a park bench, we could have just sent out invites. Evans looked around and saw the man named Patricks approaching him. The stout, barrel-chested man walked right by Evans without looking down at him or breaking his slow, leisurely walk.

Evans sighed and put his phone away before following Patricks down the path. Soon, Patricks had slowed and Evans had sped up until the two men were walking beside each other along a secluded part of the path surrounded by trees.

"You were right," Evans started first. "Steele made us the first day we started tailing him."

"Of course he did." Patricks replied with a smile. "The man was the best at what he did, and with Barris to back him, I'm surprised you were able to fool him at all."

"Well, I don't think we did."

Patricks stopped and faced Evans, looking at him right in the eyes. "Explain," he commanded flatly.

"I think he believed we were CISD, but I was getting a gut feeling, like he was holding back after our conversation at the newspaper offices." Evans reported. "I pulled surveillance back real soft on him after that, told him we were going back to Ottawa, that kind of thing. That evening someone came to his house and met with Steele and Barris. He was carrying a red folder when he went in but not when he left. The next day Barris is on the next flight out to Quebec and this guy is headed back here. I think Barris is going to start digging hard, he just arrived here in Ottawa yesterday. Still no sign of the folder."

"Where's Barris staying?"

"At a hotel downtown, checked in under his own name."

Patricks nodded. "Who's the stranger?"

Evans pulled the digital photo up on his smartphone, handing it to Patricks. "We took about three dozen pictures with a long range lens, that's the best one. No ID yet."

Patricks nodded, looking at the picture. He took a deep breath and handed the phone back to Evans.

"Do you recognize him?" Evans asked, pocketing the phone.

"Yes," Patricks replied turning down the path again. "His name is Kieran James. He's the boss's Chief of Staff." Patricks sighed. "I'll ask the boss if he can get Yim to put some men on them, if they get too close we'll just eliminate them."

"That'll be messy."

"Hopefully it won't be that messy." Patricks replied with a smile. "But we can't have them finding out what's really going on can we?"

PART TWO

ONE

Jim Barris swept his head to the right and stared at the East Block, where he knew most of the work got done, and where he would find his old commanding officer, Colonel Michael Yim. How had he gotten himself into this mess? How did he get to the place where he was standing outside the Parliament Buildings about to go in and ask questions of a high ranking military officer about the possibility of the Governor General of Canada misappropriating military personnel and equipment?

A week ago, his friend and former team-mate, Gideon Steele had asked him to come down to the small town of Forest Hills. The idea was that Jim could help train of a group of church leaders for a youth survival camping trip. Hearing about the camp, and hoping for a good ex-soldier story, a reporter named Jerry Price had gotten a hold of classified documents about Gideon's military service and that, in turn, raised some questions about some missing pieces of the document. Files that should have been there weren't.

The Governor General's Chief of Staff, Kieran James, dug into it and discovered that at least one of Gideon's "Black Operations", was approved by the Governor General, a person that was more figurehead than anything else. This raised more questions, and more and more, until questions seemed to be drowning them.

And now Jim Barris stared at the East Block, in his full Military uniform, complete with ribbons and decorations. Standing a massive six foot seven inches, with wide shoulders and narrow hips, he turned to face the Peace Tower once more and bowed his head, praying softly that Jesus would guide him today.

Jim's journey to standing here had started long before his involvement with the Canadian Special Operations Regiment. His personal journey had started in a small logging community that didn't even have a name in Quebec, north of Ile-de-Fort George, along the shores of Lac Mwakw.

Jim Barris was always a big child, standing a head or taller than the other children his age. As the son of the foreman at the lumber mill, Jim spent much of his time there, and soon grew aware of where to play, and where not to play. Jim and his friends would jump in and out of the large machines that moved the logs and knew exactly how close they could get to the huge band saws that cut them before the operator would yell.

It was an enjoyable childhood, growing up among the large trees and clear lakes of Quebec; but as Jim grew older he found that there was a larger world out there. A world full of adventure and intrigue, a world that held more than the small one room schoolhouse, and the future of working as either a lumberjack, or a lumber mill worker.

Jim's father was furious when he found out that Jim was going to leave to join the military. It wasn't the fact that Jim was leaving, or that he was joining the military, it was the fact that he had heard it from one of the workers at the mill, who had heard it from Jim's best friend, the worker's son.

Jim smiled, his Dad had been pretty mad when he confronted Jim at home that night, but Jim had made it pretty clear that he wanted out of the small logging community they lived in. So, three weeks later Jim had found himself on a train to Ottawa, where he then climbed aboard a bus to the entrance to CFB Petawawa, the largest military base in Canada, and his home for the next three months as he went through General Military Training and then General Infantry Training.

Now, twenty-five years later he stood at the base of the Parliament Buildings, the hub of government power in Canada, walking towards the East Block, where he might be able to find some answers to more recent questions

*

Gideon Steele was yawning. He slouched down in his wicker rocking chair, on his front porch and lifted the delicate teacup to his lips. The night before had been spent in a meeting with the members of the Camp Committee in charge of the Youth Survival Camp that Gideon was to be the "Survival Expert" for, and the only thing they wanted to talk about was money. How much was it going to cost them to do this, that or the other thing? Every idea that Gideon put forward the initial question was, "How much would that cost?" The majority of the answers were, "Nothing," but there were some things, the rock climbing that Gideon was sure would build confidence and the initial gear that Gideon told them they'd need would cost a fair amount of money.

In the end only a few things were agreed upon, and Gideon had waived any salary that he would have gotten in order to get those things. He was pleased, though that the rock climbing excursion that he had planned was going forward and he took a large amount of joy in that.

The committee had, however said that Gideon should attend the youth worship rally that was scheduled on Saturday, so the youth could get used to him being around. Gideon had balked at that idea at first, but Chris Taylor, the pastor of the Forest Glen Church of God that Gideon attended, said that it was an important step to having the youth trust him.

"That's all well and good, Chris," Gideon had said, "but what happens when they start asking the questions that I don't want to answer?"

"We'll cross that bridge when we get there." Chris replied.

Gideon huffed. "WE won't have to answer those questions, I will."

Gideon sipped his tea and waved at Mrs. Gable as she watered her flowers across the street. The interaction had left a sour taste in Gideon's mouth that he couldn't get rid of. The whole reason that he had avoided the youth in the first place was because of the uncomfortable questions of his military service that Gideon just didn't want to talk about. Three years ago Gideon had retired from the military as a Captain, and Special Forces assault specialist. He collected a pension that allowed him the freedom to not work and he was still young enough that he could keep himself in excellent shape. Those years had come with a price, however, recurring nightmares and a diagnosis of PTSD as well as a body that held scars both on the outside, and inside.

He noticed a plain, beige car pull onto the cul-du-sac where he lived and watched it as it pulled slowly along the road, obviously checking the house numbers. The car had no hubcaps and a radio antenna on the roof, Gideon sighed. A government car, he thought. Sure enough, the car stopped in front of his house.

A man with wide shoulders and clean, short hair stepped out and smiled at Gideon. As he walked up the front walk Gideon noticed that the right side of his jacket bulged a bit, meaning that was where he kept his side arm, and that he was a left hand shot. The awkward way the man walked also told Gideon that he was wearing a utility belt with, probably, a pair of handcuffs and a can of mace under the light half zipped jacket that he didn't need in the warm spring air.

"Gideon Steele?" the man asked.

83

Gideon nodded, keeping an eye on the man's left hand, as it worked its way into the pocket of the jacket.

"John Giles, R.C.M.P." The man pulled out his badge, in a handsome leather fold and showed it to Gideon, who frowned. "Just here to ask a couple questions about your military personnel file." The stolen file was coming back to haunt him again.

"I've already talked to the C.I.S.D. about the file," Gideon said. The Canadian Industrial Security Directorate is responsible for all the security measures put on any information or intelligence gathered by any means for Canada. They are also responsible for the investigation of any breaches of those security measures.

"Well, that may be so, sir," Giles said. "But the offence committed falls under the Security of Information Act and has to be investigated by the R.C.M.P." Giles looked confused for a moment. "C.I.S.D. should never have been involved in an investigation outside of Parliament."

"I talked to a couple officers a few days back." Gideon paused in thought and gripped his bottom lip between his thumb and forefinger. "Evens and the other guy didn't give a name just sat in the car."

"I don't know anything about that, sir." Giles smiled, as he wrote the name down, on a pad he pulled from his pocket and then placed back. He was left handed. "And I've been getting constant information from C.I.S.D. about who's accessed your file both electronically and physically."

Gideon nodded.

"We have the name of the file clerk that took your file from records, and I've talked to him." Giles continued. "He told me that he gave the first file, the one with missing reports to Kieran James, the chief of staff to the Governor General."

Gideon nodded and sipped at his tea, shoving down the familiar tang of panic in his throat.

"He also said that he found the missing reports and handed them off to Mr. James as well, gave me the date too."

Gideon's teacup shook as he placed it on the saucer.

"Mr. James flew here the next day."

Gideon clasped his hands between his knees; his morning had just gotten very complicated. "Have a seat."

*

Kieran James sat down at his desk and looked around. Nothing seemed to have been moved. Jim had told him what to look for when he got into the office, how to spot whether or not someone had been in the room looking for something. Kieran took a long look around the walls, looking for pictures, or furniture that were out of place, then moved on to his desk, examining the top of the large surface before placing his briefcase on it.

He turned to face the window and pulled back the curtain to look out at the courtyard that faced Wellington Street, a large grassed area with rolling paths and statues. He was able to easily spot Jim as he made his way to the East Block, away from Kieran's office building, where the Governor General and his immediate staff had their working areas. Jim was a large man, easily a head and a half taller than most of the tourists in the field, snapping pictures and looking at brochures.

Jim Barris had told Kieran that they shouldn't spend any time together, unless they had to meet for a very important reason. Turning down Kieran's offer to stay in his guest bedroom, Jim had instead opted to rent a hotel room and stay within a short cab ride to Parliament. Kieran also knew that Jim was hoping to have a meeting with his old Commanding Officer, a man named Randle Yim, a Colonel with the Special Operations Regiment Command.

His phone rang as he turned back to his desk and Kieran picked it up without sitting down. "Yes," he said.

"There's an R.C.M.P. officer Dowdy here to see you, sir." His secretary said.

Kieran's heart skipped a beat, and then started pounding in his chest. "Why?"

"He wouldn't say."

"Send him in." Bile was rising in his throat.

A moment after Kieran took his overcoat off and sat on the cream couch to the right of his desk, a slender man with the build of a runner walked in. Long, confident strides brought him to Kieran and he stuck out his hand with an easy smile.

"Sergeant Kyle Dowdy, Mr. James," he said. His hair was cleanly cut and his face was chiseled bare cheekbones. A moustache decorated his upper lip and it looked like he had trimmed and combed it that morning.

Kieran placed a smile of his own on his face to hide the panic behind his eyes. "What can I do for you, Sergeant?"

Dowdy pulled a ring bound notebook from the breast pocket of his jacket, revealing a hip holster with a 9mm Berretta on his right side.

"You accessed Captain Gideon Steele's military record on Tuesday of last week, correct?" he said, checking the notebook.

"I tried to." Kieran replied leaning back and nodding for Dowdy to sit. "It was restricted to me."

Dowdy nodded. "Yes, then you contacted a Corporal Mahoney in special records to get access to the physical file. Why did you need Captain Steele's file?"

Kieran shrugged. "A friend of mine asked for it."

"His name?" Dowdy pulled a pen from the same pocket that the notebook came from.

"He's a reporter," Kieran added quickly. "He was just doing a fluff piece on Captain Steele."

Dowdy nodded. "His name?" he asked again.

"Jerry Price." Kieran supplied reluctantly. He remembered Jim's advice. If anyone asks questions, answer them, but do not elaborate on anything. Answer the bare bones question. Kieran had already given away more than what had been asked for; he vowed not to do that again.

*

Jim walked into the large, wood panelled front foyer of Colonel Yim's office; he removed his head dress and tucked it under his left arm. A slightly overweight middle aged woman with a tight bun sat behind a desk that looked about to be buried under piles of folders. She looked up and smiled as he walked toward her.

"Can I help you, Warrant?" she asked politely.

"I used to serve under Colonel Yim a few years back, and I was in town. Just wanted to say hi." Jim answered with a smile. "Figured it'd be easier to catch him in the morning."

The secretary smiled amiably. "I'll see if he's available."

She stood and stepped lightly into Yim's office, barely opening the door wide enough for her body to get through. A moment later she stepped back out. "He's on the phone right now. He wondered if you could meet him out in the quad in about ten minutes."

Jim nodded and said thank you before turning back to the door. He fixed his beret properly on his head in a mirror beside the door, no doubt placed there so Yim could do the same thing before he left his office.

Jim stood by a statue of some guy from long, long ago. He sighed deeply and was just about to leave when he noticed Colonel Yim come out of the door to his office building. He had put on a little weight since Jim had last seen him, but that was to be expected, now that he was riding a desk. The beret on his head was place squarely over his immaculately cut hair, and his uniform creases were sharp and straight.

Jim smiled and snapped to attention when Yim approached.

"Stop that." Yim said with a smile. He stuck out his hand, which Jim grasped in his huge, meaty paw.

"Good to see you, sir."

"Good to see you too." Yim took in Jim's uniform, all ribbons and medals on the left side of his chest. "What's with the formal wear?"

"Thought it might make it easier to get some time with you." Jim grinned. "Besides, I hardly get to haul this thing out of the mothballs now."

Yim pointed at a Starbucks across the street. "Coffee?"

"You buying?"

"If it'll keep you from asking about the file." Yim said with a straight face.

"I'll buy." Jim replied. "How did you know that was why I was here?"

"You don't even send me a Christmas card." Yim said. "And now you show up the week after the last remaining member of your team's jacket goes missing? Come on, it wasn't rocket science."

Jim nodded. "What's up with it?"

"With what? The file or the filing?"

"Both."

"The file's still missing. RCMP are on top of it." Yim said. "The misfiling of the after action reports was just incompetence."

"What's with CISD being involved then?" Jim said. "A couple of their agents came to visit Gideon and I last week."

Yim shook his head. "CISD investigates inside of the federal government, but uses the RCMP's policing authority if they need to. They rarely leave Parliament."

"A couple of guys came down to Forest Hills. Greg Evens was one of them. The other guy was the quiet type."

Yim's face registered shock for a moment at the sound of the name, merely a flicker that Jim almost missed. Years of knowing the man and watching his reactions had taught Jim how to read Yim's face, however, and now it flashed shock, before he shrugged.

"Maybe they're not talking to each other right now." Yim offered.

Jim nodded. "What was up with the Dawson mission?" They stopped at the curb, waiting for a lull in the traffic so they could cross.

"Dawson?" Yim asked.

"B-2425." Jim replied, using the mission registration number. "The only attack that has ever been carried out on Canadian soil by the military at peacetime."

Yim shook his head and turned up the street toward a bench. "Don't go there, Jim."

Jim followed him. "With all due respect, sir, I was there and I was injured and I killed people. Did the Governor General have any input at all?"

Yim looked up. For a moment Jim saw another emotion flash across his face and just as quickly disappear. It was fear.

*

Gideon was sweating freely now as Giles sat down in the chair beside him. When he was settled into the chair, the RCMP officer laid his head back and sighed.

"I like these old chairs better than the new sling ones the stores are selling now."

Gideon nodded, surprised.

"They just feel better."

Gideon nodded again.

"I spoke with your pastor a couple days ago, when I first got this case."Giles lifted his head and turned to face Gideon. "My boss thought you were involved somehow, but my gut didn't agree. Anyways, your pastor had a lot of good things to say about you."

"He's a good man." Gideon said softly.

Giles nodded. "I read the article Jerry Price wrote about you. I admire the work you want to do with the youth."

Gideon smiled. "It's my way of redemption."

"Jesus' grace has no need of redemption." Giles said. "His sacrifice has paid all our debts."

Gideon looked at Giles, confused for a moment.

"I'm the youth leader at the church I go to." He said, by way of explanation. "I'm not here to give you trouble, Gideon. I'm just following a lead to its natural conclusion, and the trail that Kieran James left led me here. Now you either know where the file is now, or where it's gone, because I'd be willing to bet that the file was here for one reason, or another."

Gideon stared out at Mrs. Gable, who was coiling her hose. He prayed silently for guidance and wisdom, and asked if he could trust this man. At the end of five long minutes of silence, which both men were willing to wait out, Gideon felt he could.

"Kieran had this theory about one of our missions. The Dawson mission in northern Alberta." Gideon said softly.

"I remember it. RCMP took out the Dawson crime syndicate. They were involved in all kinds of illegal activity. Drugs, human trafficking, kidnapping, nasty bunch of people."

Gideon shook his head. "No, we took it out. It was a black op, off the books, eyes only type of mission. RCMP was glad for the help and we let them take the credit."

"What was the theory?"

"That it was in retaliation for the kidnapping of the Governor General's nephew." Gideon said. "The op was approved by the Minister of Defense, and was planned by myself, then Major Yim, my CO, and some guy named Patricks."

Giles had taken out a notebook and was jotting down names on the pages.

"The Minister of Defense never approves these things, he wants plausible deniability, and planning should have been done just by me and my senior NCOs. Yim should never have been there and no one had even heard of this Patricks guy." Gideon continued. "The whole thing was a mess to begin with, not to mention the whole problem of a military action on Canadian soil!"

"Where's the proof?"

"There is none, except for circumstantial and speculation."

Giles paused to take in the new wrinkle in his case. "So that was the theory, where did the file go after that?"

Gideon shrugged. "Back to Ottawa, as far as I know."

Giles stood up. "I'm going to be here until tomorrow. I've already talked to Jerry Price in person, but I might head back again. Can I call you if I have any more questions?"

Gideon stood as well. "Yes. What happens now?"

"Why didn't you question the irregularities when it first happened?" Giles asked.

Gideon shrugged. "I was a soldier. I followed orders. Now I'm a retired soldier that has a lot of time to dwell on the sins of my past."

Giles nodded and put the notebook back into his pocket. "Think about the youth, Gideon, they're the future. You can't change your past sins, but you may be able to help prevent someone else's future sins."

Gideon and Giles shook hands and Giles strolled back to his car and drove away. Gideon stood and watched as the car turned left out of the mouth of the cul-du-sac and then turned back into the house. He sat in a large overstuffed armchair and lifted the phone from the side table and called Jim Barris.

From inside the car, Giles pulled out his phone and dialed his partner, who was still in Ottawa, Kyle Dowdy.

*

Dowdy was jotting down Jerry Price's name in his notepad. Kieran was aware that they already knew that Jerry had gotten the information from him, Jerry had called after a phone interview with some RCMP officer named Giles, but they needed to confirm everything and cover all their bases.

"I want to make perfectly clear to you that passing on classified information to Mr. Price is a violation of the Security of Information Act." Dowdy said.

"There were extenuating circumstances," Kieran replied.

"Like what?" Dowdy replied.

Kieran paused, regaining control of his senses. The mention of the Security of Information Act had thrown him a little bit, but he was able to think clearer now. "I'd like to talk to my lawyer." He said calmly.

Dowdy looked disappointed and closed his notebook, realizing that he was going to get no more information for the time being. He stood and was about to say something when the door opened and Miles Doneven, the Governor General walked in.

"I'm sorry Kieran, I didn't know you were in a meeting," the Governor General apologized.

Dowdy shook his head. "No problem, sir. We were just finishing up."

Doneven examined both men closely and then smiled. "I hope it's not anything serious."

"We've yet to determine that, sir," Dowdy replied.

Doneven nodded, still examining Dowdy's face like a poker player at the table.

Kieran watched the entire exchange in horror, too scared to speak or breathe. He tried to keep an impassive look on his face but was unsure if he looked bored, or terrified, amused or shocked. So he stood silently as the two men spoke, then watched with a little relief as Dowdy turned and left the room.

"What was that about?" Doneven asked after the door was shut.

"He was asking about an old friend of mine," Kieran replied, remembering Jim's advice about not giving up information.

Doneven nodded. "Not serious I hope."

Kieran smiled. "So do I."

*

Dowdy had just closed the door to his car when his cell phone rang. "Dowdy."

"Hey Kyle, it's John." John Giles deep voice rang over the cell lines. "Just got done speaking with Gideon Steele. Nice guy."

"Hope he was more forthcoming than James was," Dowdy replied with a sigh. "He lawyered up on me when I mentioned the Security of Information Act."

"Smart move for him. He did pass on classified material."

"What did Steele have to say?" Dowdy started the car.

"Plenty, but all speculation." Giles sounded a little excited. "About some mission from a few years back, and the Governor General and the Minister of Defense being involved in using military personnel and equipment for their own purposes."

"Sounds like a Tom Clancy novel."

"He made a good circumstantial case."

Dowdy huffed. "We need proof. You know as well as I do that circumstantial means nothing in Parliament but bad press."

91

"I'm heading to the paper right now to talk to Jerry Price again," Giles said. "What's your plan?"

"Think I'll go to talk to Mahoney's Sergeant. I want to know all the procedures for dealing with these files."

The two men said goodbye and Dowdy started his car. It sputtered at first and then started with a roar. Carefully pulling out of the lot he drove the three blocks to the special records building, a large, windowless box that looked like a warehouse with new siding.

It took him ten minutes to pass the three security checkpoints where his car was searched for bombs, his body was x-rayed and his sidearm handed over for logging, no one, except security personnel were allowed to carry firearms, even if they were federal cops.

When he finally got to the front desk and asked for Sergeant Bailey of Special Records, the civilian receptionist informed him that Sergeant Bailey had been reassigned to Germany.

"I'm just looking for an explanation of procedures for filing and storage of sensitive material." Dowdy explained. "Can I speak with the CO, or someone else that can help me?"

The receptionist nodded. "We just had a new Commanding Officer start up yesterday. I'll see if he has time."

The receptionist picked up the phone and dialed a few numbers. "Colonel Patricks, please."

*

"Why on earth would you think such a thing?" Yim asked, sounding incredulous.

"Just following the breadcrumbs," Jim replied. "The Dawsons took the Governor General's nephew, held him hostage and for ransom. When they got the ransom, they killed him anyways, and sent the pieces home. It's pretty common knowledge that the Minister of Defense and the Governor General work closely with one another and it was George Barkley, the Minister of Defense himself that approved the op in the first place! Since when does the Minister himself approve Black Ops?"

Yim stared at Jim for a moment and then turned to head back to the building his office was in. "You're one crazy, Frenchman, you know that Barris," he said with a chuckle, his face turned away, but somehow Jim was sure that there was fear on it again.

Jim's phone rang in his pocket. "I'll catch up in a minute, sir."

"Don't bother, Chief Warrant Officer Barris, I think we're through for today," Yim replied.

Jim frowned and hit the call button. "Yeah."

"Pleasant answer you have there, Ox," Gideon's voice said.

"Less than pleasant visit with the old CO."

"What's up?" Gideon sounded concerned.

"I think he's involved somehow," Jim replied.

"Yim?" Gideon sounded shocked now. "No way!"

"He's hiding stuff and he's trying to cover up stuff," Jim muttered, walking back towards a cab stand by the entrance to Parliament. "He also recognized your friend Evens' name."

Gideon was silent a long time. "You want me to come up there?"

"No, it's a waste of time," Jim replied. "I'm coming back. I'll meet with Kieran and tell him to keep his head down, but without some serious weight we're not going to get anything."

"That's why I called," Gideon said. "The RCMP's involved now."

Jim smiled. "Well then let me talk to Kieran, get back to lovely Forest Hills and let the Mounties do their job."

*

Colonel Patricks was a slender man, in his prime he might have been called an Olympic level athlete, but now, in his late forties, he was starting to develop the rolls and sags of a man past his prime. Graying hair and a heavily creased face told of a man that had seen it all and lived to tell the tales. However he was not allowed to tell many of his tales.

The phone in his pocket, the "special" phone, rang and he casually reached in for it.

"Patricks," he said efficiently.

"It's Doneven," the Governor General said. "I just left my Chief of Staff's office where he was being questioned by the RCMP."

Patricks nodded. "And. . ."

"And what?" Doneven almost yelled. "The RCMP is involved now. I called Barkley and informed him, and he told me that when he tried to get a hold of Yim this morning, he was out having coffee with a Warrant from one of his old units."

Patricks eyes narrowed now. "We know that Barris is in town, it's conceivable that he would try to get information from his old CO."

"Will Yim talk?"

"No, Yim knows to keep his mouth shut." Patricks said. "He's been in since the Dawson thing, so he'll keep quiet now. And we have leverage on him."

"Their probably talking charges on Kieran James for violation of the Security of Information Act," Doneven said, his voice was calming now, his mind beginning to work.

"He'll try to bargain his way out," Patricks said. "He'll have to go. Barris too."

"Agreed," Doneven said. "I'll let Barkley know. Can you get Evens and his boys moving?"

"Don't tell Barkley," Patricks said. "Don't want too many hands in the pot, and it's best if at least one of you has plausible deniability."

There was a moment of silence. "It's a pity," Doneven said sadly.

"What?"

"Kieran was a good Chief of Staff."

Patricks hung up and sighed before turning to his computer and calling up the number of Evens' latest burner phone that he used. The phone on his desk rang this time, and he had to suppress the urge to snarl into it as he answered.

"There's an RCMP officer here to ask you some procedural questions, sir." His receptionist said.

TWO

Colonel Patricks watched from his office window as Officer Dowdy of the RCMP drove away. He had been thorough. A lot of questions were asked and a lot of answers were given. He had taken up most of Patricks morning and things were well on their way to lunch now when the phone in his pocket rang again.

"Patricks," he said, less than politely.

"It's Evens. I've got everything ready for Mr. James. All I need is a crowded, public place to give it to him."

"Follow him," Patricks replied. "I'd like to see that the problem is dealt with tonight."

"And Mr. Barris?"

Patricks frowned. "He's going to be more difficult. We'll have to be careful with him."

*

Gideon opened the front door and smiled. Sara Michaels stood on the front porch in a red and yellow sundress, her brown hair shifting softly in the spring breeze and her wide brown eyes looking up at him. She smelled faintly of some kind of sweet perfume that he couldn't place.

"Good evening," she said in her soft voice.

"Come on in." Gideon held the door wider for her automatically glancing out at the street beyond and seeing just the regular cars on his street. "I ordered Chinese for dinner."

Sara laughed. "Are you ever actually going to cook for me?" This was the fourth time Sara had come to Gideon's for dinner and each time he had ordered out for them. Greek, Thai, and Italian, now Chinese.

Gideon shook his head. "I like you too much for that."

Sara smiled and shook her head as she walked into the house and sat on the couch. Gideon followed sitting in the plush chair across from her.

"Are you going to the youth meeting on Saturday?" Sara asked.

Gideon shrugged. "Thinking about it."

"It's important that the kids get to know you," Sara said. "They need to get to know you so that they can learn to trust you."

"I know all that stuff," Gideon replied, sounding frustrated. "But there are some questions that I'm sure will come up that I just don't know if I can answer."

"I haven't asked you a question yet that you haven't been able to answer."

Gideon shrugged his big shoulders again. "You aren't a kid. I remember being a kid, and looking for adventure and glory, and thinking that Rambo and James Bond were the paragons of men."

"Then tell them they aren't."

"You're making this way too simple."

It was Sara's turn to shrug her shoulders. "I'm sorry if you want it to be more complicated."

Gideon grunted.

"Sounds like you're worried that they'll look up to you because of your past. You need to make sure that they look up to you despite your past."

"And how am I supposed to do that?"

"Keep doing what you're doing," Sara replied with a smile. "You've already gone too bat for this rock climbing thing. You're already helping them achieve experiences that will build character and confidence. You are going to be more impactful in their lives just by showing them that they can achieve things that precious few people three times their age have."

Gideon nodded, thinking about Sara's words. The front doorbell rang and Gideon got up to answer it. It was the food and after he paid he brought it back past the living room to the dining room where he laid it out on the maple dining table.

Sara followed and helped set the table, as they filled their plates, she said, "I'll be around to help anyways."

"What do you mean?" Gideon asked as he spooned lemon chicken onto his plate. "On Saturday?"

"No, on the camping trip," Sara replied as she pulled the disposable chopsticks apart. "There has to be a medical professional there too. Insurance requires it."

"Sounds like the insurance company is running this thing more than we are," Gideon muttered. "How much is the insurance going to cost?"

"Don't you worry about that. You just worry about keeping everyone safe."

Gideon sighed. "That much, eh?"

"That's why everyone was so worried about cost at the last meeting." Sara said between mouthfuls of food. "You eased a lot of stress when you turned down a fee."

"I don't need money," Gideon said.

Sara smiled. "Another reason why your help is needed."

*

Kieran James wandered into the crowded dining room of the Copper Kettle. It was dim and pressed with people that were drinking and laughing after working at Parliament all day. A few blocks from the famous buildings it was a favourite stop of most of the junior staffers on their way home. A place to relax and wind down before the drive home to sleep and do it all again the next day.

He was surprised to get the text from Jim on his cell phone asking to meet here for dinner, only two days after being told to not contact unless it was an emergency. Kieran's nerves were raw all day, and he was jumping at every strange noise he heard. A trolley of mail had banged into a wall and he almost ducked under his desk in front of his secretary while they finalized the next day's agenda.

He saw Jim's big six foot seven inch frame sitting at a table that seemed too short for him, and relaxed. He smiled and pushed through a crowd of people that were waiting for drinks at the bar. The Beach Boys were playing on the speakers, how long had it been since Kieran had taken a vacation? He couldn't remember.

There was a bump of someone touching him, and a couple people stepped one way or another to try to make room. Then there were three sharp pains in his side that travelled up to Kieran's chest. He suddenly found that he couldn't breathe. He took a step, but his legs wouldn't work. He tried to fall forward but, instead fell into another person, who glared at him for a moment before seeing the blood trickling from his mouth.

Kieran slowly slumped to the ground. The pain in his chest was all consuming. Someone stepped on his hand but it only registered as a slight pressure on his fingers. He heard someone scream but couldn't make out words. There was something sticky under his body as he tried to move, roll over, anything. Then he decided to rest a moment and try again in a bit. He closed his eyes. They never opened again.

*

Jim saw the surprise in Kieran's eyes and thought someone had stepped on his foot. He watched as Kieran stumbled forward into someone and then was shocked as blood started to trickle from the corners of his mouth.

Jim stood immediately and scanned the room. A middle-aged woman saying she was a doctor was pushing toward where Kieran was falling, a small area had cleared around him now and when the woman was able to push into the clearing she stepped on his hand. Jim looked out to the fringes of the crowd and saw no one rushing away from the scene. As he passed the crowd, the lingering scent of sweat and fear hung in the air.

Jim now turned and looked around in a circle, moving towards the door as he did. If someone had come to the restaurant to eliminate Kieran, the name "Jim Barris" would also be on that list.

As Jim neared the door, someone from the crowd yelled, "He's been shot!" Jim stepped out and onto the sidewalk, turned and walked steadily away from the restaurant.

He took the first two rights and the next left before he heard the sirens. The blocks were small and he was impressed with the response time of the local police. He took the next left as well, moving away from the scene.

He figured most people wouldn't remember his face, but it was his size that would be the problem. There just weren't that many six foot seven men walking around in the restaurant, even with the commotion of Kieran bleeding on the floor. He looked down a couple alleys as he walked and found a homeless person sitting on the concrete by a dumpster. He offered the man sixty dollars cash to go into a convenience store and buy a pre-paid cell phone. When he returned Jim said he'd give the man another one hundred dollars. When the surprised homeless man returned with the cell phone, Jim handed him 160 dollars and asked for the man's ragged blanket and beat up Senator's hat.

He wrapped the blanket around himself, hunching over to just over six feet and looking and smelling homeless. Jim glanced around and took a series of random corners as he tore the packaging off the cell and ditched them in three different trash cans along with the crumpled remains of the bill. He opened his personal cell and pulled out the sim card, snapping it

98

between his fingers and dropping the two halves down separate sewer grates, he tossed the remains of his phone in a trash can. Only when he was sure he wasn't being followed did Jim dial Gideon's home on the pre-paid cell.

*

"I'm telling you," Gideon said. "I don't own a T.V." He bunched up a bag of the Chinese leftovers and opened the cupboard under the sink to throw it in the garbage.

Sara looked shocked. "Everyone has a T.V., Gideon."

"I don't," he insisted with a smile. "You can search the house if you like."

The phone on the wall beside the fridge rang and Gideon pulled it up to his ear. "Hello?"

"Kieran's dead."

Gideon's heart dropped. His joy and relaxed mood as he talked and joked with Sara was gone in the second and a half it took to say two words. He immediately recognized Jim's voice. He would know it if he was almost deaf, so he could also assume it was true. Jim was too good to report information he wasn't sure of.

Sara was suddenly concerned as she watched Gideon's face drop and his shoulders hunch over, resting his bald pate on the door of the fridge. She took a few steps closer to him, unsure what to do.

"How?" Gideon asked.

"I have no clue. One minute he's walking toward my table and the next he was there lying on the ground bleeding all over the place. No gun shot, just blood. My guess is a knife of some kind."

Gideon nodded. "What's your plan?"

"I'm not even going back to the hotel," Jim said. "I'll be back to you in the morning, not sure how yet, but it'll happen."

Gideon nodded. "Take care, Ox."

"You too, Cap."

Gideon hung up the phone and turned to face Sara, who was looking worried.

"What's wrong?"

"We need to talk," Gideon said as he gently lead her to the living room.

*

Jim shoved the phone in his pocket and started down the street. His

99

head was slightly down with the peak of the hat high on his forehead so he could look out under it, but it appeared that his eyes were focussed on the sidewalk.

He wandered along a few side streets until he reached a sidewalk where the light was red. He waited patiently, his mind mulling over his next move.

Ottawa had become too dangerous for him to stay, if they came after Kieran, it would only be a matter of time before they came after him too. Whoever "They" were.

Heading back to his hotel was out of the question, they would know where he was staying, it was only a matter of calling hotels in the area and asking for Jim Barris. In hindsight he should have used a fake name, but he was a soldier, not a spy.

I'm a soldier, Jim thought, a soldier of God. As the light turned green, Jim started to pray.

"Lord," he muttered in French as he walked. "I need a direction. What's my next move? Please be with Kieran if he lived. Please have mercy on him if he didn't. He was trying to do the right thing." He paused as a couple took a wide berth around the big muttering man in the threadbare blanket. He smiled. "I'm kind of new to this praying thing, Lord, so any help would be nice right now."

He looked ahead and saw a convenience store. Coming out the door was a man carrying a bag of milk. It took a moment for him to realize it was the pastor that had led him in the Sinner's Prayer two days ago. Jim stood to his full height and stared in shock at the sixty year old man a mere five feet away.

The pastor stopped at the curb and looked in Jim's direction and after a moment of confusion, recognition bloomed on his face.

"Jim?" he said.

"Hello, Pastor Kyle," Jim replied. "I think I just got schooled in the power of prayer."

A few moments later the two men were standing on the porch of Pastor Kyle's house, three blocks from the store.

"So you need to get to Kitchener?" Pastor Kyle said. "No questions asked? You realize that you sound like you're running from something."

Jim smiled and nodded his head. "I know that's exactly how it sounds, sir. But it's actually a little more complex than I'm willing to get into right now."

"You make it sound like some kind of James Bond double-oh-seven type of deal." Pastor Kyle tilted his head and looked at Jim appraisingly for a moment. "You some kind of spy?"

"James Bond has gadgets and a gun." Jim replied with a grin. "I have a thirty dollar cell phone and a stinky blanket."

Pastor Kyle chuckled, and nodded. "There's a truck driver that goes to the church," he said. "He's headed to Windsor tonight. Has to be there by 8 AM. He can probably drop you off in Kitchener, that's not too far from Forest Hills, isn't it?"

"I can get a lift from there."

Pastor Kyle went inside to call his friend and Jim took out his cell phone and called his hotel to arrange to have his belongings sent back to Quebec. After he finished that call he immediately called Gideon.

*

Officer Dowdy was pulling into the driveway of the condo he rented when his cell phone rang. He sighed and left the engine running as he picked it up.

"Dowdy," He said, less than politely.

"Kyle, it's Greg." Greg Driver was Dowdy's commanding officer and head of the Parliament Investigations Group in Ottawa, responsible for any crimes committed on Parliament grounds or involving Parliament personnel. Because of the sensitive information that most Parliament employees were privy to, the R.C.M.P. took all their cases seriously, no matter how trivial they may seem.

"I just got home." Kyle muttered.

"Sorry," Greg said. His voice was tense. "That guy you were looking into earlier today about the missing file?"

"Yeah, Kieran James, he's the Governor General's Chief of Staff. I'll write up the report in the morning. I also saw a Colonel Patricks over at the Records facility, just to get a feel of how the records are kept."

"James was just shot dead at The Copper Kettle, a restaurant a few blocks from Parliament."

Kyle was silent for a beat as he took in the new information. "I know the place. I'm on my way." He hung up, dropped the cell phone in his pocket,

101

flipped on his flashing lights and pulled out of the driveway.

It took him only a few minutes to reach the restaurant. Police cruisers had blocked off the street entrance and were providing a blockade for anyone that was trying to get a look at the show. Kyle wove his way through the crowd and flashed his badge at the uniformed officer standing on the inside of the yellow tape stretched across the street.

As he approached the door, he paused and pulled his cell phone out again and dialled John Giles, his partner that was asking questions in Forest Hill about the missing file that had started this whole mess.

"Giles." The deep voice came from the speaker at his ear.

"Hey, it's Kyle," He said. He stepped towards the blood stain on the floor. The body had been taken away. "Kieran James is dead."

"What?" Giles said. "What happened?"

"I don't know I just got here now. But your circumstantial evidence is starting to look pretty good."

"Jim Barris went to Ottawa with James after he met with Steele."

"He may be another target," Kyle muttered, as he waved over a uniformed RCMP officer. He covered the mouthpiece with his hand. "Find me a man named Jim Barris, he should be at a hotel somewhere around Parliament," he said to the officer.

"Steele might be a target too, I'll check on him," Giles said before he hung up.

Kyle placed his phone in his pocket and looked down at the stain. "Any witnesses?" he asked the officer that had escorted him into the crime scene.

"Plenty that saw him die, none could tell you what happened, though," The officer replied.

"So, everyone stood around as the Chief of Staff of the Governor General was shot three times and no one saw anything?" Kyle said, turning on the officer. "Someone, saw something, find that person!"

The officer turned and headed towards a back room where the patrons were being kept and interviewed by more uniformed RCMP officers. Kyle turned and stepped back outside, where he pulled his cell phone out and dialled the coroner's office.

"This is Inspector Dowdy with the RCMP, has Kieran James body arrived yet?" he asked, waiting for the terse reply. "It'll be there soon, when it gets there everything gets dropped and his post-mortem is done ASAP."

Kyle smiled as the coroner on the other end said something loudly into his ear.

"He was the Chief of Staff for the Governor General," Kyle said with a grin. "Would you like to answer to him why there aren't any answers about his Chief of Staff's death yet?"

*

Gideon hung up the phone and turned to face Sara.

"That was Ox," he said softly. "He's on his way back. I'll have to pick him up in Kitchener in about 6 or 7 hours."

Sara was staring at the floor, she nodded.

"Say something, please," Gideon added.

Sara took a deep breath. "So there's a file out there about you that someone doesn't want to get out. Now that it's out, there could be some danger to you, right? I mean since someone has killed this other guy."

Gideon smiled slightly. "It's a little more complicated than that, but yeah, that's the basics," he said with a chuckle.

Sara frowned and looked up at Gideon. "No, you don't get to make fun of this!" she said vehemently. "This whole 'life and death' thing may have been common to you at one time, but this is all new and very unwelcome territory to me."

Gideon looked down to the floor, ashamed. "It's unwelcome to me too, I'm sorry."

There was a long pause before Sara's eyes softened. "I'm not mad at you, Gideon. I'm . . . I don't know, just mad in general about the entire thing."

Gideon nodded. "I am too."

Sara's eyes became worried. "What are you going to do?"

Gideon sighed, "I'm going to pick up Ox in about 6 hours. Then we'll plan the next move."

"What about the kids?" Sara asked. When Gideon looked at her, confused, for a moment she added, "If you're in danger wouldn't they be in danger if you're out in a forest somewhere?"

Gideon nodded. "That's one of the moves we'll have to plan."

"It's kind of an important part of the plan," Sara urged.

103

"In my head there's nothing more important than the safety of those kids," Gideon said, looking directly into Sara's eyes. Sara smiled, somewhat frightened.

THREE

Kyle Dowdy stepped into the Coroner's examination room. It smelled of sharp bodily fluids and disinfectant. The whole room made him wonder what type of people would work in such a slaughterhouse.

The Coroner was a man in his early fifties. Kyle had heard of him but had never actually met the man. It was said that he preferred to work the night shift, and listened to classical music as he cut into his patients. He strode over to Kyle with confident steps and his pale, thin hand held out. He had dark, almost black hair, with only the hint of graying along the temples. A high widow's peak adorned his forehead and a closely cut soul patch was the only facial hair on an otherwise neatly shaven face.

"Good evening Inspector." Dr. Lloyd Chase said, with a genuine smile.

Kyle shook the hand, which was cool, but firm. "Have you started the Kieran James post yet?"

Chase nodded. "I have. I've found cause of death, which is, not surprising. Three puncture wounds to the lower back, angled upwards into the thoracic cavity. Whatever made the wounds were small, perhaps 2 centimeters in diameter the weapon was thrust upwards at about a 50 degree angle, causing catastrophic damage to Mr. James' lungs and heart. I also found a powdery materiel in the wounds. I collected some for you." Chase reached into his pocket and pulled out a small glass jar with a sticker marked "evidence" in red letters.

Kyle took the jar and signed the sticker on the jar and a clipboard that Chase handed him, indicating that he had received the evidence. "So he didn't even have a chance?"

Chase shook his head. "None at all. The wounds were small, but the damage done to his lungs and heart were fatal. His life after the attack would have been measured in seconds."

Kyle shook his head, as he looked at the body, covered head to toe with a sheet. "Poor guy."

Chase turned to face the body as well. "Sooner or later, everyone takes a rest on my table," he said, philosophically.

Kyle looked at Chase with a wry grin. "You're an odd man, Dr. Chase.

Thank you for your insights and your speedy work," he said as he pocketed the small jar in his coat pocket. "Let me know if anything else comes up."

Chase smiled back, as if he was used to the comment. "I shall, Inspector."

*

Sara had gone home three hours earlier. Gideon was sitting in his favourite plush chair and staring out the window into the night. He prayed and asked for guidance, wisdom and a number of other things, but nothing came to him, no answer. His life was moving forward, good church, good friends, and then, BANG! his past crept up and ambushed him from all sides. Maybe he should cancel the camping thing. That was a lot to ask, the thing that made his life better, which was to heal his heart and his soul. How could he give that up? He had fought helping with the camping trip at first, but now it felt like he couldn't go on without it.

He tried to forget the things he had done, tried to ignore the nightmares, and the panic attacks, but he couldn't. He prayed and he studied God's word, and that helped, but still the panic crept in and the nightmares invaded his sleep. He sighed as he looked at the clock again. It was time to go get Ox.

A car pulled right into his driveway as he locked the front door. As the driver door opened Gideon recognized the car as Inspector Giles'. The RCMP officer stood and peered at Gideon from over the roof of his car.

"Going somewhere?" Giles said with a smile.

"Got to pick up a friend," Gideon replied.

"Would that happen to be Jim Barris, coming in from Ottawa?"

Gideon nodded. "Just picking him up in Kitchener, off the 401."

"Did you hear about Kieran James?"

Gideon made his way down the steps as he approached the passenger side of Giles' car. "Ox is worried that he's next."

"Ox? Barris?"

Gideon nodded. "Been calling him that for years."

"He should be worried," Giles paused. "It's also occurred to me that Barris might be the killer."

Gideon shook his head. "Someone would have remembered a 6'7" man killing someone else in a bar."

"He was a highly trained soldier." Giles countered.

"He was a soldier, not an assassin or a spy."

Giles considered that statement for a second, then asked, "Where are you picking him up?"

"You going to arrest him?"

"Not unless I can prove he's broken the law," Giles said, "I'm a cop, not a vigilante," he added with a smile.

Gideon stared at Giles, examining him. Control was flowing out of his hands. RCMP involved, high ranking government officials were involved somehow. Kieran killed in a crowded room, Ox on the run from everybody. Who could Gideon trust besides Ox and Sara? and Sara wasn't prepared for what was going on. Everything was leading to the past, back to Gideon and Ox's involvement in something that had happened years ago, with the Dawson mission. But that didn't answer the question who to trust.

Gideon took a deep breath and then noticed a glint on Giles lapel, a flash of moonlight reflected off a gold pin. It was a cross.

"You drive," Gideon said as he pulled open the passenger door.

Giles was surprised at the sudden statement and fumbled with the door handle. "Okay."

*

A thin man in a black turtleneck was sitting in the passenger seat of a rented, black Suburban. His eyes were glued onto the event taking place in the driveway four houses down and across the street. Gideon Steele and the RCMP officer Giles were talking over Giles' unmarked car. Suddenly the two men got into the car and pulled out of the drive. The thin man waved a hand towards the unmarked RCMP vehicle and a large, burly black man with cauliflower ears pulled out behind them at a discrete distance.

The thin man pulled a cell phone from his pocket and hit a speed dial number, the only one in the memory.

"You were right, Steele left just now. A little late for a milk run, don't you think, sir?" The thin man's voice was soft and breathy, like he was reciting poetry as he spoke.

"We knew Barris was heading back to Forest Hills." Patrick's voice returned. "It was really the only play left to him after James was killed. Follow them and deal with the two of them."

"That Mounty Giles is with him."

There was a long pause. "Do you have enough men to deal with all three?"

"I have four men with me, sir." The thin man said with a smile. "All assault specialists."

"Good," Patricks replied. "I look forward to a positive report."

"Yes, sir." The thin man stuffed the phone back into his pocket and turned to the three men in the back seat. "Gear up."

*

The man that Pastor Kyle had arranged to give Jim a lift to Kitchener was named Mitch Stone. He was overweight and his arms were covered in tattoos, he said they reminded him of who he used to be before Jesus had saved his life and his future. Jim immediately liked him. Mitch went on and on about how Pastor Kyle had lead him to a new life, and a better life. His wife and kids loved him now, and he no longer drank or partied. He enjoyed his life now, instead of feeling like he was constantly missing something, he felt like he was constantly being blessed with something.

The two men talked for about an hour before Mitch mentioned that Jim could catch a quick nap if he liked. Jim was suddenly reminded of the words that his training Sergeant had said to him one afternoon. "If you don't have to run, walk. If you don't have to walk, stand. If you don't have to stand, sit. If you don't have to sit, lay down. If you don't have to stay awake, sleep." So Jim leaned back into his seat and let the rocking of the big truck lull him to sleep.

It seemed like only a moment before Mitch leaned over and shook Jim awake and said they were nearing Kitchener.

"I'll pull off at Homer Watson and let you off there," he said, "There's a Micky D's there that makes pretty good coffee," he added with a smile.

"And maybe a quarter pounder?" Jim asked returning the grin.

"Or two," Mitch said, slapping his big belly with a laugh.

Jim laughed and sat up straighter. He had ditched the old blanket and hat at some rest stop along the way, so all he really had on him was his wallet, some keys and the clothes on his back. He scanned the area where Mitch would let him off, looking for danger areas, or "kill zones" where a sniper could take him out from 500 meters away. The land was wide open and flat, with only a few buildings around. A gas station, the McDonalds that Mitch would soon enter and a Tim Horton's were nearby. All low buildings with few people around at 3 o'clock in the morning.

Gideon was supposed to meet them in the parking lot of the Tim Horton's, a customary meeting place for any Canadian. Jim didn't like the poor lighting in the lot, but that couldn't be helped and it was no better than any other lot around.

Mitch left Jim by the side of the road directly across from the Tim Horton's and smiled, saying he enjoyed meeting him and to keep in touch.

"God bless you, brother," Mitch said with a smile as Jim closed the passenger door.

"You too," Jim replied with a wave.

He watched the transport pull into the McDonald's and park far from the door, then he crossed to the Tim Horton's, looking forward to buying a double double and a carrot muffin. With the coffee shop on his left and a field on his right he saw Gideon's big frame standing beside a car, near the back of the lot. A man Jim didn't recognize was standing beside him and the two were talking. Gideon lifted his hand and waved Jim over, then pointed at the car and mimed drinking out of a cup.

Good old Cap, always prepared. Jim thought.

To Jim's left a car parked and two men got out. One stepped from the driver's seat and the second got out from the seat directly behind the driver. Odd, Jim thought. The driver turned awkwardly to close the door with his left hand, while keeping his right arm stiff and pointed down. The man coming from the rear seat stood with his door opened and looking around the parking lot. Not good, Jim added to his previous thoughts. A shadow moved slightly from the field beside the parking lot, carrying what looked like an MP-5.

"Gun! Gun! Gun!" Jim yelled as he ducked and ran.

Gideon was suddenly in motion and rolled over the hood of the car he was leaning on. The man Gideon was talking to pulled a hand gun from a shoulder holster, Jim vaguely noted it was in his left hand as he started running at the car, weaving between the few cars in the lot to provide some cover. The attacker from the field fired a few times, but Jim knew it was just to herd him into an area where the men that were now coming out from behind the car could get a clear shot.

Gideon started to open the driver's side door and slip into the car. Giles moved to the rear of the car and took a couple shots at the men moving towards Jim.

Jim elected to run towards the building and hunker down by a brick wall.

*

Gideon jammed the car in drive and reached over to force the passenger door open as Giles fired three rounds towards the man attacking from the field.

"Get in!" Gideon screamed, bile rising in his throat, his heart starting to pound in his temples.

Giles folded himself into the car and Gideon stepped on the gas before the door was shut. He pointed the car straight at the two men stepping out from behind the car that Jim had been watching earlier, then suddenly turned left, towards Jim's hiding spot, as they scrambled to either side.

Giles had opened his window and was trying to get a shot at the man that was running to Jim, while reaching for the hand radio mounted under the dash with his free hand.

"Headquarters, Charlie Two, Two. Shots fired at Homer Watson and 401, at the Tim Horton's parking lot. Request immediate back-up!" Giles roared into the mike.

"Stopping." Gideon said, as he slammed on the brakes in front of Jim.

The back windshield erupted as gunfire shattered it. A few rounds struck the dash, creating small explosions of plastic. A sudden thumping and crashing came from above them and the roof caved in slightly. Giles dropped the mike and pointed up at the roof with his gun.

"What was that?" Giles yelled hysterically.

Three thumps came from the roof.

"Big crazy Frenchman on the roof," Gideon muttered as he slammed on the gas.

The car ripped forward towards Homer Watson. The gunman from the field stepped out and peppered the hood with his weapon. Gideon and Giles ducked down and the car clipped the gunman, who waited too long to jump away.

Gideon's foot eased off the gas as they pulled onto the road.

"Keep going. It's an RCMP car," Giles said, "The hood is armoured. It'll run."

"I'm not worried about that," Gideon said as he looked into the side mirror. When he saw the gunman they'd clipped roll over on his own, he sped up again. "I was making sure he was okay."

"What do you care?" Giles muttered. "He was trying to kill us!"

"I've killed my fill," Gideon said softly. He looked into the rear view mirror and saw Jim sliding his way, feet first into the back seat. He heard, vaguely the noise of the radio saying that Waterloo Regional Police were on route, and Giles saying that he was on route to headquarters with witnesses.

"I should have stayed in Ottawa." Jim muttered.

"Welcome back, Mr. Barris," Giles said with a grin.

"Who's the cop?" Jim asked as he turned to look at Gideon.

Gideon's hands were white on the steering wheel. His head was shaking slightly and he was taking quick, sharp intakes of air.

"Cap, pull over," Jim said softly. "Switch seats with me."

Gideon pulled over, bumping over the curb roughly. Jim stepped out and Gideon rolled into the back seat. When Jim climbed back in he slammed the seat back as far as it would go and pulled off again.

Jim angled the mirror so he could see Gideon lying on the backseat, amongst the shattered remains of the rear window.

"So, who are you?" Jim asked Giles, as he kept an eye on his friend and another on the road.

"John Giles, RCMP." Giles replied looking back with worry in his eyes. "He gonna be okay?"

Jim nodded as he pulled onto a small side road and took the first right.

"Let me guess, you're the official investigator for the missing file and not the CISD agents that we met last week."

"They should never have even been here." Giles nodded. "What's he muttering?"

"He's praying."

"Should I?"

"If you like."

Giles twisted in his seat as Jim turned down another dark road and laid his hand gently on Gideon's knee.

"Father," he prayed, "be with our friend, Gideon. Give him your endless reserve of strength and fortitude. Let him know your love for him, and your plans for him. You have everything under control, and everything that is happening is happening according to your will and your plan. You are gracious, Father. Please show Gideon your grace. You are merciful, Father.

Please show Gideon your mercy. In Jesus' precious name, amen."

Giles sat forward again and stared out the passenger window into the darkness.

From the driver's seat, Jim nodded.

*

Jim pulled the car to the side of the road about 15 minutes later and shut it down. Gideon was sitting up again and breathing steadily, staring out the window with his hands resting lightly on his lap.

"Cap, you remember corporal Robert Graves?" Jim asked, looking at him through the rear view mirror.

"One of the assault guys from Squad 3, right?" Gideon replied as he scrunched his face up to remember.

"Yeah, when Shaw broke his leg, Graves subbed for him for a couple of missions," Jim said, "He was also the guy you hit with the car."

"Is he still serving?" Gideon asked.

Jim shrugged his big shoulders.

"I can find out," Giles said reaching for the radio under the dash. "Now I know why they put these things so low, less likely to get shot."

"Headquarters, Charlie two-two," Giles said into the radio.

"Go ahead," a woman's voice crackled.

"Can you run a name for me on the military database? Name Robert Graves, no D.O.B."

"10-4."

A few moments later the dispatcher's voice returned. "Charlie two-two. Sergeant Robert Graves, D.O.B. 01-23-1985. Regular force, active. The rest of his file is classified."

"Thank-you, headquarters, 10-4." Giles returned the mic to its holder and turned to face Jim. "Well, he's still on active duty."

"So what's he doing here?" Jim asked.

"Who was his Commanding Officer?" Giles asked. "We could ask him."

Gideon shrugged, "No clue, we were pretty compartmentalized."

Giles nodded. "Let's head back, I'm going to set you two up with a security detail and we can track down this Graves guy there."

Jim looked back at Gideon in the rear view mirror and waited for him to nod before starting the car and driving off.

Giles smiled and shook his head before pulling out his cell phone and calling his partner.

"Dowdy," he heard. Kyle's voice sounded tired.

"How soon can you get to Forest Hills?" Giles asked.

"Are you kidding me?" Kyle snapped. "I haven't even stepped into my house since 0700."

"Get a cruiser to drive you down." Giles replied. "I have Jim Barris and Gideon Steele here and someone just tried to kill them, and me."

"Waterloo Regional Police is gonna love that." Kyle muttered. "Fine, I'll get there ASAP."

"I'm gonna get a protection unit on them as soon as I get back to Headquarters in Waterloo," Giles said. "We also have a name for one of the shooters."

"Tell me when I get there." Kyle hung up without another word, jammed his car into reverse and backed out of his driveway.

*

Soon Jim was pulling into the RCMP headquarters in Kitchener, ON., a large, brick building with great steel and glass doors at the front entrance. Giles directed Jim around the building to the back parking lot. There he guided him to a spot under a floodlight, and motioned Jim and Gideon to stay put.

"I'll be right back," Giles said as he opened his door and stepped into the light around the car.

Gideon and Jim looked at each other and Jim shrugged his shoulders. Giles stepped to a painted green, steel back door and rapped on it with the side of his fist. The door opened and a few words were quickly exchanged. After the animated conversation Giles waved for Gideon and Jim to come in.

The corridor was made of concrete and cinder blocks. The three men wound their way through a labyrinth of halls. When they appeared at a small, unmarked door Giles opened it and beckoned the two men inside.

"I'll be back in a moment," He said as he waited for Gideon and Jim to enter.

"We'll wait in the hall," Jim said, suspicion in his eyes.

Gideon touched Jim on the arm. "It's okay.", and he walked through into the bare room.

Jim followed him into the room and scanned around. A large mirror filled most of one wall and a simple metal table that was bolted to the floor sat in the centre. Two metal chairs were on either side of the table. A video camera was mounted in the far corner of the room, no light was on, and so Jim assumed it was off. When he turned to try the handle of the door he found that it turned easily and opened, no one was in the hall.

"That's a relief I guess." Jim muttered.

Gideon sat one of the metal chairs and looked up at Jim. "Let's take stock of our situation."

Jim grabbed the other chair and spun it around, sitting on it backwards and resting his arms on the chair back. "The file that was supposed to be classified and buried was taken from the special records depository and is now wanted by people that remain unknown to us."

Gideon nodded. "People that are connected to the government, are using government assets to retrieve the file. But why the whole smoke and mirrors thing with the CISD agents? Why not just use actual agents?"

"Because they couldn't?" Jim offered. "Or maybe because CISD agents aren't trained to do what they wanted them to do if they found the file?"

Gideon nodded. "They couldn't use them is more likely, I think. Probably because these unknown people only have control of a specific section of the government." Gideon paused. "Given that Graves is involved, and is still active within some unit, we can safely assume that the section of the government in question is the military."

"Which makes me think that this whole attacking us, and killing Kieran is being done without the government's knowledge."

"So Giles' investigation and the RCMP involvement is legitimate?"

Jim shrugged. "How should I know? You're the officer."

"We'll assume he's legit, for the moment," Gideon said with a smile. He began to relax a little, the familiar banter back and forth with his former senior NCO making him feel safe, "So to clarify, unknown people within the government are using military assets to retrieve a file, and kill civilians associated with said file, all without the rest of the government's knowledge."

Jim sighed, his big shoulders sagging. "Well, when you put it that way," then he shot his head up. "Wait a minute, you said military assets."

Gideon nodded.

"Only military personnel have access to military assets." Jim continued.

114

"So who, within the government has access to military assets?"

"Minister of Defence and the Governor General are the highest ranking. And the Governor General is just a figurehead." Gideon said. "Could be thousands, though."

"But how many would have access to units as elite as the one that Graves is in?" Jim replied. "Also, the Governor General may only be a figurehead, but in reality he really does hold a lot of power. He could, if he wanted to, access the military units we're thinking of."

Gideon nodded. "That still leaves us with a short list," he said.

"Crap!" Jim yelled. "We're idiots!"

"We're maybe a little slow at times. . ." Gideon started, confused.

"No!" Jim cut him off. "Do you remember that first night when Kieran brought the file over?"

Gideon nodded.

"He pointed out the Dawson mission."

Gideon slapped the palm of his hand into his forehead. "It was approved by the Minister of Defence!"

"And Kieran pointed out that the Dawson's had kidnapped and murdered the Governor General's nephew a few months before." Jim added.

Gideon suddenly looked shocked. "We're talking about the Minister of Defence and the Governor General, misappropriating military assets for personal use."

"And that surprises you?" Jim laughed. "How many bayonets do you have at home?"

"No, these are people's lives!" Gideon suddenly stood and shot his chair back. "We killed people based on a lie!"

Jim took a deep breath; and nodded. "We did," He said softly.

FOUR

Gideon and Jim sat in silence for a few minutes, trying to accept the thing that they had done. The Dawson mission had been the only military action they had ever taken on Canadian soil. A relatively simple assault, that went anything but simply.

Yet here it was, rearing its ugly head again. And now there were more casualties.

"So let's run with this theory." Gideon said softly. "The Governor General uses a covert assault force to kill off the Dawsons."

Jim nodded. "Given the evidence, it's plausible."

"What was the reason given for the assault in the orders? I can't remember." Gideon asked, rubbing his chin.

"Standard crap," Jim said with a smile. "In the interests of National security."

"What about the corroborating investigation?"

"Near as I can remember there wasn't one." Jim added.

Gideon looked confused for a moment. "There wasn't an investigation? Or there wasn't a file with the findings in it?"

"Don't know the answer to that one," Jim replied. "All I can tell you is that there was no investigative file attached to the orders that Kieran had."

"There must have been some kind of investigation to prove the threat against the security of the country." Gideon said, rubbing his forehead now.

"Wouldn't you have seen it when you got the orders and planned the assault?"

Gideon shook his head. "I wouldn't have needed it. By the time it got to the planning phase it should have been followed up six different ways by ten different people. Then it got sent to the authorizing officer and then down the chain to me."

Jim stared at his hands for a moment, then looked up to Gideon and smiled. "What if the operation started with the authorizing officer and skipped the corroborating investigation?"

"Then the corroborating investigation file wouldn't exist."

"But it should exist." Jim confirmed.

"Yes," Gideon nodded. "And it should be attached to the file that we saw, because there would be only one hard copy of that order, we shredded any copies of files we had after missions."

"But it wasn't." Jim started to smile. "This means that what we saw was a copy and either there's another file out there that has the investigative report, or there never was an investigation done."

"And if there was never an investigation done," Gideon took up the line of thinking with a smile. "Then the authorizing individual, in this case the Minister of Defence, would be misappropriating military personnel and equipment."

Jim nodded soberly. "And the death of forty five civilians and two good soldiers,"

Gideon sat in silence for a moment. "Where's the file now?" he asked.

"It's safe." Jim replied.

Gideon looked up and stared at Jim's face for a moment. "You have it on you?"

"Good thing I don't play poker." Jim muttered as he reached down to his calf. Gideon heard the sound of tape ripping and then Jim placed a plain brown envelope encased in a Ziploc plastic bag on the table between them.

Gideon stared at it for a moment. "We probably shouldn't tell anyone about it until we have some kind of security that we won't be prosecuted for following orders."

Jim nodded. "Odd that such a small thing can have such a huge impact on people's lives."

They stared at the small package in silence, each lost in their own thoughts and memories. Gideon reached out and touched a corner of the bag. "Vengeance is mine, I will repay, says the Lord." he whispered softly.

"Huh?" Jim grunted.

"Romans 12:19." Gideon replied, he looked up and smiled. "Look it up in the Bible you stole from my place."

Jim shrugged. "I was going to give it back when I could pick one up."

"Keep it, I've got lots."

"It's in my hotel room in Ottawa now." Jim replied. "Assuming it's not been tossed by someone yet."

Gideon nodded. "It probably has been."

"We're in it deep, aren't we?"

"We've been here before." Gideon replied. "This time we have faith and the Lord."

"So did all the disciples." Jim muttered.

*

The phone rang at 5:06 AM. Pastor Chris Taylor rolled over and grabbed it, glancing once at the clock. His friend and parishioner at the church he pastored, Gideon Steele, would call it, "stupid o'clock". Chris smiled at the thought.

"Hello," he whispered into the phone, looking over to make sure his wife was still sleeping. Calls at this hour were usually not good news for a pastor.

"Pastor Taylor?" the voice on the other end had an official tone to his voice. "I'm sorry to call you so early," he continued after Chris had confirmed his identity. "My name is Sergeant Grey of the RCMP. We have a teenager here who asked us to call you. He's 18, so he has the choice. His name is Fredrick Cross?"

"Fred?" Chris said, sitting up and stepping out of the room. "Is he okay?"

"He's fine," Grey replied. "Our narcotics unit busted a crack house about two hours ago and he was picked up outside it, on the street. He says that he was there waiting for a friend. His friend was picked up in the house."

Chris nodded. "I'll be right down to pick him up."

"You can come down, but he hasn't been cleared yet."

"Thanks." Chris grabbed some clothes and checked on his sleeping wife. She had gotten so used to the late night\early morning calls that she was still asleep. He said a quick prayer for her, and scrawled a note to leave on her bedside table, and then he silently crept out of the house.

When he had left, Tina Taylor sat up and grabbed the note, quickly scanning it. She crumpled it up and dropped it onto the floor before she lay back down, releasing a sigh.

*

Giles stalked the corridors of the RCMP building with a worried expression on his face. He was able to acquire a safe house to hide Gideon and Jim in but there was no manpower to provide a security detail for them, so he had made a couple calls to Toronto for help. He had also turned off the cameras and microphones in the interrogation room that he had placed

119

them in. He wanted, desperately to know what they were talking about, but he also had to earn their trust. He wanted to work with them in this problem, hopefully to find a solution to the questions that just kept on coming up at every turn.

As he turned the corner a small thin man in a wrinkled polo shirt and jeans bounced off his chest and would have fell, if Giles hadn't reached out and grabbed him. Giles noted the man was wearing running shoes, with no socks.

"Woe there!" Giles said with a smile. "Where are you headed?"

"Sorry," the man said. "I'm Chris Taylor, I'm looking for the cells. One of my friends has been arrested, I just got the call."

Giles studied the man for a moment. "Do you have your visitor's ID?"

"Oh! Sorry!" Chris said as he stuck his hand in his pocket and pulled out a red "Clergy" visitor's pass."

Giles studied the ID and handed it back. "I'll take you, pastor."

The two men walked down the halls and Chris told Giles the situation with Fred Cross. Giles took it all in and smiled, as he opened the door to the holding area.

"He should be fine, pastor," he said with a nod. "As long as his friend from in the crack house corroborates his story."

"He shouldn't have been out with people like that anyways." Chris said with a frown.

"My pastor always says that the only way to heal the sick is to meet the sick." Giles replied.

Chris thought for a moment about that. Then he nodded and walked through the door.

"I'm looking for Fred Cross. He was brought in a few hours ago." Chris said to the overweight officer at the desk, as he clipped the clergy ID to his collar.

The officer looked down at a clipboard in front of him and said, "He's up in Interrogation Room One."

"What?" Chris yelled. "He hasn't been charged with anything, has he?"

The officer at the desk shrugged. "I'm sorry, padre. All I do is keep track of where they are."

Chris sighed and headed back out the door, looking around for any signs that might lead him to the interrogation area. At the elevators he saw the RCMP officer that had helped him find the holding area. He was talking to another uniformed officer.

"Excuse me?" Chris said as he approached them.

The big man that had helped him smiled. "Hi, Pastor Chris. Did everything work out for you?"

"Not really." Chris muttered. His face was starting to flush. "They have him in an Interrogation Room!"

The uniformed officer held up a hand. "Slow down, pastor! I'm Sgt. Grey, the guy that woke you up. We're just keeping him up there until his story can be confirmed. It's on the second floor, there's signs to point the way."

Chris paused, then rubbed a hand over his eyes. Taking a deep breath to settle himself he said, "I'm sorry. Please forgive me."

Sgt. Grey smiled. "No apologies necessary."

Chris turned to the officer that had helped him earlier. "Thank you for your help. I didn't even ask your name."

"Sgt. Inspector John Giles." Giles replied. "We spoke on the phone a few days ago."

Chris smiled like a light had gone off in his head. "That's why your voice sounded familiar! Why didn't you say something before?"

Giles shrugged. "You seemed a little frazzled."

Chris nodded and chuckled. "Yeah I guess I was."

"I'm heading up that way right now." Giles said with a smile. "I'll take you."

The two men said goodbye to Sgt. Grey and stepped onto the elevator. Giles pressed the button and after the doors closed they started to move.

"I've got to admit, I was shocked when I heard there was a crack house in Forest Hills." Giles said shaking his head. "It looked so," he paused, searching for the word. "Small townish."

"Apparently small towns make good distribution centers." Chris said gravely. "They bring shipments in from various points and distribute it from there. North, south, east and west. Forest Hills is pretty much in the middle of Ontario, from where we are they can move their goods anywhere."

"You seem to know an awful lot about it." Giles laughed as the doors opened.

"We have a few ex-dealers at the church." Chris replied. "I make it a point to get to know each and every person that comes to Forest Hills Church of God."

"Sounds like you have quite the problem here." Giles said as he led Chris down a plain, cream coloured corridor with doors down the right side. Uniformed guards were at three doors.

"The bigger problem is that there aren't enough cops to get the job done." Chris said as he stopped at room number one. "The dealers actually outnumber the cops."

Giles stopped and examined Chris for a moment, then nodded once and turned towards the last room in the hall.

Chris looked at the guard and showed him the pass on his collar. "Just want to chat." he said, sadly he had done this before.

The guard nodded and opened the door.

*

Giles knocked twice and opened the door to the interrogation room where he was hiding Gideon Steele and Jim Barris. As he walked into the room he noticed the two men facing each other as if they had just been calmly chatting. He also noticed a Ziploc bag filled with sheets of paper on the table between them. The bag had not been there before and it was too large to have been in either man's pockets.

"Hi guys." Giles said with a smile. "Been writing your memoirs?"

Gideon shrugged. "We're just trying to decide if you were a good guy or a bad guy." The pounding in his chest was starting again. His breathing wanted to run out of control, but he wouldn't let it. His palms started sweating.

"I just wanted to know if you wanted something to eat." Giles smiled.

Gideon smiled and took a deep breath. This was getting too much. Too much stress, too much of his old life. Silently he nodded.

"Sounds like a good idea." Jim said with a smile. "Coffee too, please. Then we'll go over our memoirs,"

Giles nodded and stepped back into the hall.

FIVE

Patricks lifted the "special" phone to his ear as he waited for the coffee to finish brewing. He was wearing his uniform, minus the jacket for the moment, and was taking the lid off the travel mug that he would bring to his new office.

"Yes," Only a few people had this number, and he was expecting a call about the operation in Kitchener.

"It's me, sir." Patricks recognized the voice of the thin man in the black turtle neck.

"Is it done?"

"There's been a complication, sir." The thin man said. "They were able to evade us; there was another man there as well. He was driving an unmarked police vehicle."

"Are you sure?"

"I've seen enough, sir." The thin man paused to take a deep breath. "Graves was injured. Our medic says that he might have a broken pelvis. He's not mobile."

Patricks thought a moment. "We need to clean house. Dump Graves and get back here,"

There was a long pause. "Sir?"

"You have a problem fuollowing orders?"

"No, sir," came the immediate reply.

"He was my boy before he was yours." Patricks said as he casually poured coffee into his travel mug. "I don't like this either. Make it painless."

"Yes, sir."

Patricks hung up the phone and sat at his breakfast table, took a sip of coffee and then dialed another number on his special phone.

"Hello." Minister of Defense George Barkley said.

"We have a problem." Patricks said. "Steele and Barris are still alive and we can assume they have the documents. We need to tie up loose ends; anyone that wasn't there in the beginning."

Barkley thought for a moment. "That would be what four or five people?"

"Yes, sir." Patricks said, taking another sip of coffee. "A few new boys on the team and Colonel Yim."

"You sound like you've already got this planned." Barkley laughed.

"I do, sir. I've had contingencies for this planned since the beginning. That's why you brought me in, planning and execution."

"And you're very good at it." Barkley said. "The documents will prove nothing, right?"

"Some bad press, sir." Patricks replied. "They'll need talking people to get proof."

"Carry out your plan, Colonel."

"Thank you, sir." Patricks hung up the phone and shouldered his jacket, just another day at the office.

*

Giles was headed back up to the interrogation area after picking up some breakfast and coffee from Tim Horton's. He carried a large paper bag and a cardboard tray with three extra large coffees in it.

Chris walked out of Interrogation Room One as Giles approached it. He glanced down at the bag and the coffees. "You went on a coffee run and didn't ask me?" he said with a smile.

"Sorry, it's for some important guests we have here." Giles said. "How's your friend doing?" He tried to change the subject.

Chris shrugged. "As well as can be expected, I guess. He was trying to convince his friend that he didn't have to stop at the crack house, and after was just waiting for him to come out to try to convince him that he didn't need to take the drugs."

Giles shook his head. "Sad," he muttered. "Where are Fred's parents? Why did he call you?"

"He lived with his grandmother until her death when he was 14. She brought him to our church; she taught him how to live life properly. After her death, Fred moved in with his parents, they're both alcoholic, druggies. He's basically been raised by adults at the church since then."

Giles was saddened, and he looked down at the floor. "Guess it's bad everywhere, even here."

Chris nodded, and then smiled and slapped Giles in the shoulder, "If you're still here on Sunday, drop by. Service starts at 10:30 AM. I'll be taking Fred home in a few minutes, they say he can go. His friend spoke up for him."

"Well that's good news for Fred." Giles looked up and smiled back, but there was little joy in it. "If I'm still here on Sunday, I'll be there."

He turned and trudged down the hall, opening the door to Gideon and Jim's room. "I bring gifts of food and caffeine." He said with a broad grin.

Gideon and Jim descended on the food like they were starving. Giles noticed that the Ziploc bag that was on the table before was now under one of Jim's thick legs. He deliberately ignored it, figuring that sooner or later they would mention it.

When they were finished eating, Jim leaned over and clapped Giles on the shoulder, "Thanks for breakfast." He said with a smile and a laugh.

Gideon rolled his eyes and sighed. "Yes, thank you." He said. "You probably want to know what's in the bag, right?"

Giles nodded. "It had crossed my mind."

Jim lifted his leg and handed Giles the plastic bag. As Giles opened the Ziploc portion he scanned the first page through the clear plastic. His eyes widened, he reached in with trembling fingers and pulled out the thick sheaf of paper.

"Is this. . ." he started.

Jim nodded. "It's the missing documents that Kieran James took from the secured documents vault." Jim stood and paced back and forth in the room for a moment. His huge strides ate up the room quickly. "He gave them to me to keep safe when we landed in Ottawa. I had them taped to my leg when I went to the Copper Kettle to meet him the night he was killed."

"Wait!" Giles exclaimed. "You were there?"

Jim nodded. "I watched him suddenly fall. I don't know how and I don't know who, but I can tell you that it has something to do with those files right there." Jim pointed at the files in Giles' hand.

Giles stared at him.

"If you read those you'll see that they are after action reports and authorization orders for each of our 'black operations'. If you're careful, you'll also note that each order has an attached 'corroborating investigation' report, that's to ensure the validity of a threat to national security before you order a black op." Gideon explained. "Operation B-2425, has no investigation report. If you're really good, you'll note that the authorizing officer is always a Colonel, rarely a General, B-2425 was ordered by the Minister of Defense himself."

Giles was now staring at his lap. "The Minister of Defense?"

Jim started talking now. "The operation he's talking about was the Dawson Compound assault. The Dawson Boys were actually responsible for the kidnapping and brutal murder of the nephew of the Governor General, a close friend of the Minister of Defense."

Giles nodded. He was starting to get feeling back in his brain and following along with the line of thought that Gideon and Jim were laying out. "The theory is that the Governor General asked for help from the Minister of Defense and you were sent in as payback for the death of the nephew."

Gideon shrugged. "That's the theory, unfortunately that's all we have is a theory, no proof."

*

Colonel Randle Yim was the son of Chinese immigrants that had moved to Canada in the early '60s. Shortly after their immigration, in 1968, Randle was born; he was named Randle because it was a strong "western" name. His parents had raised him bi-lingual and to cherish the beauty of their homeland, but to also love and respect the land that they had made their home. The Yim family had started a small restaurant in Vancouver, and it prospered, so much so that by the time Randle was 10 years old they enrolled him in private school and he excelled in academics and sport. His parents were never more proud of him than when he graduated as valedictorian of the private high school he had attended and then went on to enroll the next day for the Royal Military College in Kingston, Ontario.

The separation had been hard for them, but as was expected of him, Randle had excelled. He graduated near the top of his class and went on to advanced tactical courses and eventually to lead a platoon of the Special Operations Regiment.

He had first met Colonel Patricks when he was a Major, and still leading the small team that he had built by hand picking the men under him. The team was, in his mind, unstoppable, but when he met Patricks, that all changed. Patricks was known as a "troubleshooter", a member of the military that answered only to the Minister of Defense, and the file that he had slapped on his desk was registered with the "B" prefix, B-2425, a "black op". Yim had hated those, because they were dangerous and there was never any backup for his boys, no matter how hard he yelled. Moreover, Yim noted right away that there was no "corroborating investigation report",

126

which didn't sit well with him.

Patricks had told him that the order was directly from the Minister of Defense and above investigation. Yim balked and said that he needed the investigation report to make it legal, he also noted and mentioned that the order was for combat action on Canadian soil, something that he had never done.

"Look Yim," Patricks had said. "The usual team that we get to do this stuff is overseas right now. Your team is more than qualified to go in, do the job and get out. No press, no muss, no fuss."

"Sir," Yim started. "If I take action on this without an investigation report, we'll all be hanging out in the breeze."

"You let me worry about that, Major." Patricks leaned in closer, the pores on his face visible to Yim's brown eyes. "By the way, how are your parents doing in Vancouver these days?"

Yim stood straighter and took a tentative step back in shock; were his parent's just threatened?

Patricks smiled. "Your reply is, 'Yes sir, I'll start the planning right away.'"

"Yes, sir," Yim muttered without feeling the words. "I'll start the planning right away."

Now, all those years later he stood in the small kitchen in the loft apartment he rented in Ottawa, a cup of coffee in his hand. He felt as if he had sold his soul to the devil, a devil named Patricks. What bothered him more, was that the Minister of Defense and the Governor General were both involved too. He had done his research and figured out the connection with Miles Doneven and his nephew, he had even amassed a few "questionable" black operations that had been carried out by one of the other spec ops teams in the regiment, always the same team, always no investigation report, always ordered by either Patricks, or George Barkley, the Minister of Defense.

He thought absently about the safe deposit box in Vancouver where he had hidden copies of the files and orders and wondered if he should move them. A flash of light caught his eye from the building across the street, he recognized it as a reflection from a sniper's scope immediately, and dove to the ground just as a .300 round shattered the window of his kitchen above the sink and burst his microwave into a thousand pieces. Yim soldier crawled to the cupboard under his sink where he kept a Glock 9, a handgun that shot 9mm rounds that were sure to stop anything that would come at him.

Running crouched to his front door he checked the weapon to make sure it was loaded and flipped the safety off. The front door opened with a bang as two men rushed into the room, they were surprised to see Yim running at them with a weapon and as Yim fired and dropped prone, they fired at the space where he once was.

Both men fell. Yim pulled himself back to his feet and checked the hall. He was panting and sweat was starting to bead on his forehead. He was getting to old for this. He reached down and pulled the goggles and neoprene masks from the attackers. Fear gripped his chest. He started panting harder. Sweat started to flow freely.

Yim recognized both men as being in Patricks' questionable unit in spec ops. One was Sergeant Greg Evens, and the other was Corporal Martin Mays. Both men were now dead, and lying in Yim's doorway, a door opened up the hall and Janine Taylor, one of Yim's neighbors stuck her head out.

"Call 911!" Yim yelled at her. She ducked back into her apartment and Yim hurried towards the stairway, stuffing the Glock in the jump pocket of his combat pants. He was supposed to be inspecting the sniper training school in Petawawa today, so he was wearing his BDUs, Battle Dress Uniform. Guess he was really going into battle today.

When he got down to the parking garage he took a quick look around, sirens were blaring outside and he knew that there was no way he could make it out of the garage without being stopped. His government issue ID might have gotten him through, but that was upstairs on his dining room table, along with his wallet and car keys. Stupid, he thought, I'm getting to old for this!

He rushed over to one of the fire exits and burst through it into an alleyway. The fire alarm started wailing and Yim walked as casually as he could out into the throng of people on the street. He even thought to look up, confused, at the building he had just exited.

"Nothing to see here," he muttered softly to himself. "Just an Army Colonel, with no ID wearing Combat BDUs and carrying a loaded Glock that just killed two people." He chuckled softly, causing a couple people around him to look and stare. "Nothing. Just a funny joke I was thinking about." He said to them, and then turned up the street, farther from his apartment building.

Patricks had done this. Yim was sure of it, the men were Patricks' and that was proof enough for him. The question now was where did he go? Where was it safe for Yim? There were only two other people in the world that knew about the file B-2425, Jim Barris and Gideon Steele. He needed to get in touch with them. Jim had just been in town the day before, but that was before Kieran James was killed in the middle of a bar a few blocks from Parliament, the man that had started all this mess was dead. It was safe to assume that Jim was in the wind now. So that left one option, get to Forest Hills, and Gideon Steele.

*

Chris was allowed to take Fred home, but he dropped him off at the home of an older couple from the church. Fred was tired and scared and feeling a little sheepish that he had been arrested for trying to talk his friend out of going into a crack house. He had just parked his blue Caravan in his driveway when his cell phone rang. He took a deep breath and lifted the phone, thumbing the answer button at the same time.

"Hello?"

"Chris? It's John Rogers." Christ was about to ask how he was doing when John suddenly spoke again. "Where is Gideon? I was supposed to meet him at his house this morning to go over the budget for the camping trip?"

John was the chairman of the board of directors for the Church of God in Canada, and the man responsible to the individual churches in the country for the funds and how they were spent. The camping trip was supposed to be a youth retreat that was designed to build character and confidence in the young people. Gideon was supposed to be the survival expert that the insurance company wanted.

"I don't know, John." Chris replied. "I'm sure he has a good reason to have missed it. He's usually pretty much punctual to the second."

"Well he should be here." John sounded like he was getting angry. "I'm sitting outside his house at ten o'clock in the morning!"

Chris shrugged and smiled. John was nearing eighty years old, but you wouldn't believe it if you saw all the work he did. "Calm down, John. Like I said, I'm sure Gideon has a good reason."

*

Kyle Dowdy was chugging down his fourth coffee of the trip as he pulled off the 401 onto Homer Watson Boulevard. His cell phone rang from its holder on the dashboard and the caller ID indicated it was his partner, John Giles.

"Hey, partner." Kyle muttered. "Get a good night sleep?" He lifted the Tim Horton's cup to his lips.

"Jim Barris had the files." Giles said bluntly.

Kyle nearly dropped the cup and swore. "I'm too tired for jokes, Giles."

"I'm not joking, he just handed them over to me, along with a theory that the Minister of Defense and the Governor General conspired to use Canadian Special Operations Forces to make a hit on Canadian Citizens under the guise of National Security threats."

Kyle was speechless. He started with a thought that he wanted to say, or a question, but the only thing that came out of his mouth was, "I'm ten minutes out."

When Kyle arrived at the RCMP Headquarters in Kitchener/Waterloo, he leapt out of the car without locking the door and flashed his badge at the security station impatiently. Giles had told him where he was keeping Barris and Steele, so he followed the signs down to the interrogation rooms.

He knocked once on the door and then walked in. Jim Barris was sitting in a chair that seemed two sizes too small for him across from another man, who made the chair seem only one size too small. He assumed the second man was Gideon Steele. John Giles was sitting in a third chair around the table, it looked like at any moment they would start playing cards.

"Hi, Kyle." Giles said.

Kyle frowned. Jerk, he thought, two can play this game. "Deal me in, boys." He smiled.

Jim looked at Gideon and grinned. "Oh, I like this one already, Cap."

"You would." Gideon smiled back.

Kyle turned and grabbed another chair from the hall and placed it on the remaining side of the table, he didn't like that his back was to the door, but he figured that Giles, who was across from him would keep an eye out for him.

"I called Greg Driver already." Giles said. "Told him the whole story."

"Well, tell me too." Kyle muttered. "I was out getting popcorn during the beginning of the movie."

Giles filled in Kyle about the theory that Jim and Gideon had laid out for him a few hours earlier, The two big men interrupted briefly at times to correct, or add details and in a few minutes Kyle had the whole story.

"That's pretty weak." Kyle said. "But it answers a lot of questions, like why Kieran James was killed."

"He was the first one to come up with the theory." Gideon said. "We were so used to following orders that we didn't question the missing investigation until we looked at it closely."

"Also, we didn't know about the kidnapping of the Governor General's nephew until Kieran told us." Jim added.

Kyle leaned back in his chair, "Where are the files now?"

Jim patted his right leg with a hand the size of a basketball. "Safe. Turns out you have tape here."

Kyle shook his head. "I don't want to know." He looked at Giles with a concerned face. "What's our next move?"

"We wait." Giles replied. "Greg's going to get us a warrant for the Investigation Report for B-2425. If it can't be produced, then we go ahead and arrest George Barkley for misappropriation of Military personnel and equipment, also for the murder of forty five civilians and the wrongful deaths of 2 military non-coms."

"Still going to be a tough one to prove." Kyle said. "We need someone to talk."

"Colonel Yim was downright scared when I asked him about B-2425." Jim said. "He knew the operating number too." He looked at Gideon. "When was the last time you knew the operating number for any of our ops?"

"Never," Gideon replied. "The only reason I know this one is because we've been concentrating on it so much."

"I'll give him a call." Kyle said. "But first I need a few hours of sleep."

Giles nodded. "We should have a safe house in an hour or so, at least that's what I was told."

"So more like three hours." Kyle frowned.

SIX

Colonel Randle Yim was standing in front of the large row of lockers at the Ottawa Train Station. He knew that one day he would be deemed no longer useful to Patricks, and that he would have to move in a hurry. He had rented out one of the lockers for the last 10 years, ever since the disastrous Dawson mission.

He opened the locker door and pulled out the canvas gym bag out onto the floor. He carefully locked the door again and headed to the washrooms, where he locked himself into one of the stalls and opened the bag. Inside were a couple changes of clothes, a warm jacket and a wallet with two thousand dollars in hundreds. The wallet also contained ID that identified him as Randle Wu, a driver's licence, OHIP health card and a birth certificate, all master forgeries made by a government employee that owed him a favour.

Randle changed into the casual polo shirt and jeans that were in the bag and placed his uniform inside, zipping it up and slipped the wallet into his back pocket.

A few moments later he was standing in line to get a ticket to Kitchener, Ontario. He was hoping to meet up with Gideon Steele, since he was almost certain that Patricks would have already killed Barris. He sighed deeply as he thought of the big man. Barris was a good soldier, one of the best that had ever served under him, and one of the best men that Randle had ever known.

How would he be remembered? It was just a matter of time before Patricks caught up to him, so would he be remembered as a soldier, or as a man that sold out on his friends, on his teammates, on his brothers? He didn't really have a choice, did he? Patricks would have killed his parents! The maniac had threatened them right in his own office!

After the Dawson mission it had been worse, though. Patricks wanted to keep tabs on Randle, and had created small "jobs" for him to do. Make sure that this man was transferred to this unit, or make sure that this equipment was ready to go to here. He had always been paid for the service, but that only made it feel worse, like he was making a deal with devil to keep his

133

parents alive. No mention had ever been made about them again, that almost made it worse, the waiting, the imaginary scenarios, the imaginary deaths.

Randle bought his ticket under the assumed name and sat down on a bench in the concourse to wait for his train. His eyes scanned everywhere, he had to wait for an hour or so before he could board, and he hated being out in the open. He had deliberately picked a bench against the wall, but still the sheer number of people walking around him made his heart beat a little faster. It reminded him of combat, and his adrenaline started to surge. He took a deep breath to calm his nerves and started scanning each face he saw, looking for a tell, looking for someone whose eyes drifted and stayed on him a little too long. Scanning, scanning, always scanning.

He spent the next hour, almost motionless looking at people as they passed, and when the announcement came that his train was boarding, he was surprised. Lifting the gym bag he boarded the train and found a seat at the back of the car. He took an aisle seat and placed his gym bag on the window seat, if he had to move it he would, but not before someone asked him.

The train pulled away, and for the first time since he was in his apartment, Randle Yim, now Randle Wu, relaxed a little. He also knew that this wasn't over; he needed to find Steele, and try to fix the problem that he had caused ten long years ago.

*

Kyle Dowdy was spent by the time he entered the front door of the safe house that was arranged for Gideon and Jim. He followed the three RCMP officers and the two big witnesses into the front foyer of a single story, three bedroom house in Fergus, a few kilometres down the road from Forest Hills.

He dropped his suit jacket over a chair by the door, he knew that in a few minutes one of the officers would be sitting in that chair, guarding the door.

A blue cube van was sitting in the driveway, inside were four members of the RCMP surveillance and tactical squad down from Toronto. Giles had set it all up while Kyle was driving to Kitchener/Waterloo. Kyle nodded to himself and took a few steps into the house. A large living room with a couch and a couple of club chairs was sitting to his right, on his left was a long hall that ran to the three bedrooms. Kyle looked down the hall, the walls were bare and covered with wooden paneling, which he knew covered a half inch of steel.

Gideon dropped his huge hand on Kyle's shoulder. "Don't take this the wrong way," he smiled. "But you look like crap."

Kyle chuckled. "Been a rough couple days," he said. "And I haven't slept since yesterday morning."

"So go sleep." Jim said. "By the way, where's Giles?"

"He's just finishing some paperwork." Kyle replied as he pulled off his tie. "He should be here in a couple hours."

Jim nodded and walked over to a bookcase in the living room. He started scanning the titles. Gideon started down the hall and stepped into one of the bedrooms.

"Aren't you tired?" Kyle asked Jim.

"I'll be tired later." Jim replied as he pulled out a book with a black cover. "Cap and I already talked and I pulled first watch. I'll wake him in four hours."

"So what's good reading to stay awake?" Kyle smiled and pointed at the book in Jim's hand.

"The Bible." Jim replied and sat down in one of the club chairs.

Kyle nodded once and turned back down the hall, headed to one of the two remaining empty rooms.

Jim watched Kyle head towards the room and wondered if he was a Christian. He didn't think so, but he was still so new to this and wasn't sure if there was a handshake, or some other way to tell. Some of the reading that he had done in the New Testament made it clear that he was supposed to show love to everyone, regardless of the condition of their souls, but there was a part of him that wanted to meet more Christians, if only to talk to them.

Gideon, whom he liked to call Cap, was a Christian, but he had told Jim to find other people to learn from, that he didn't know enough himself to answer all the questions from a new Christian.

Suddenly Jim realized that he hadn't even told Cap that he had accepted Christ while he was in Ottawa. Everything had moved so quickly when he got back, that there wasn't any time to talk about it.

One of the RCMP officers was sitting in the chair by the front door, reading a hunting magazine, the other two were in the kitchen, looking like they were getting ready to play a game of cards. Someone had put on a pot of coffee, and a thirty something year old brought in a mug.

"Would you like a cup of coffee, sir?" he asked.

Jim shook his head. "No thank you, and don't call me 'sir', most people just call me Ox."

The officer smiled and nodded, reminding Jim of a grandson, listening to his grandfather's story for the thousandth time.

Jim sighed and opened the Bible. He was getting too old for this stuff.

*

Gideon laid down on the bed and didn't even bother to take his shoes off. In the car he asked if there was a phone, the officer that was driving said that each bedroom had a separate line with multi channel sequencers that would make tracking the call virtually impossible. Gideon chuckled at that, but he had to call Sara and let her know he was alright. She would have already heard about the fire fight at the Tim Horton's, and she knew he was going there to get Jim.

He lifted the phone and heard a number of clicks before the dial tone. He waited as Sara's cell rang and rang, then was picked up by her answering machine. He smiled at the sound of her voice.

"Sara, it's Gideon." he said after the tone. "I'm safe, so is Jim, the RCMP have us somewhere safe now, until this can be worked out. That's all I really have right now. I'll call again tonight. Take care."

He hung up the phone, feeling a little better just for hearing her voice on the machine. He set the phone back on the bedside table and stared at the ceiling. Had he lied to her? Was he safe? If these people could get men from his old unit to come and try to kill them, what else could they do?

*

Giles dropped the Officer's Report into the inbox of the desk sergeant and wandered back towards the side door where he had parked the replacement car he had been given, since his first car was now evidence. A young officer in uniform ran up from behind him and grabbed his arm.

"Sorry, Inspector, but there's an urgent call for you." the young officer said.

Giles hung his head and asked who it was.

"Waterloo Regional Police."

Giles wandered back into the busy work room and grabbed a phone off one of the desks, the inspector at the desk looking up at Giles with narrowed eyes.

Giles ignored him and pulled up the line that the young officer had told him.

"Sergeant Inspector Giles." he said into the phone as he smiled at the frowning Inspector, who turned back to the file on his desk.

"Hello, Inspector." The voice on the other side was a deep rumble. "This is Detective Bains with WRPD. You had a BOLO out on Robert Graves?"

"Yes," Giles stood straighter and smiled. "Did you find him?"

"Well, kind of."

"What's that mean?"

"His body was found in a motel just of the highway on King Street." Bains said. "We just got the hit back on his prints, your BOLO was attached."

"Cause of death?" Giles asked.

"Single 9mm gunshot to the forehead." Bains replied. "Also had a broken pelvis." He waited a beat. "Why did you want to speak to him?"

"He was involved with the shootout at the Tim Horton's this morning, according to an eye witness I have." Giles said, rubbing his eyes. "I can also tell you that his pelvis was broken by my car as we escaped from the attack."

Giles could hear the detective scribbling notes on a pad. "Yeah I had you on my list of people to get together with today, and then this call came in from the motel. Maid found him."

"I'll forward you my report." Giles said. "Everything's in there."

Giles also gave the detective his cell number if he had any more questions and then hung up. He wandered back to the parking lot a second time, still in a daze, another lead had dried up. He knew they would have to find a person willing to talk if they were going to catch these people that were using the government as their own hit squads, these people that felt that they were above everybody else and that rules didn't apply to them. Giles was going to make sure to drop the rules right on their heads.

But first he had to get to the safe house and sleep.

*

Giles stumbled into the safe house in Fergus about an hour later. He signed in with the officer at the door, and made his way to the living room, surprised to see Jim sitting in a club chair, reading what looked like a Bible. He dropped into one of the club chairs and smiled as Jim looked up at him.

"Can't sleep?" Giles asked.

"Nope." Jim said. "I'm on guard for another couple hours."

Giles frowned. "That's why we have the guys outside and the three in here."

"Don't bother, inspector," one of the officers playing cards in the kitchen called. "We've tried. He's nothing if not dedicated."

Jim smiled, and shrugged his big shoulders. "Just providing backup."

"What are you reading?" Giles motioned to the Bible.

"Proverbs." Jim said with a smile. "I was told it's good to read one every day. I've got a lot of days to catch up on."

"I'm the youth pastor at the church I go to in Ottawa." Giles said and leaned back in the club chair. "I tell the kids it'll give them wisdom. You'd be amazed at how some kids that seem so smart, just don't want wisdom."

"Same thing goes for adults too." Jim said with a smile. "Go get some sleep, Giles. You're no good to Cap and me if you're falling asleep while someone tries to kill us."

Giles was silent for a moment and Jim thought he might have fallen asleep in the chair. Then Giles frowned a little. "Waterloo Region Police found Robert Graves."

Jim nodded and stuck a massive finger in the Bible to hold his place. "Is he in custody now?"

Giles shook his head, no. "He's dead. A maid found him in a motel, shot in the head."

"Cap isn't going to like that."

"I don't like it." Giles replied standing and starting towards the bedrooms. "We're running out of leads."

*

Randle Yim had gotten off the train in Toronto, even though his ticket was straight to Kitchener. He rented a car in his fake name and drove the remaining distance into Forest Hills. It was almost four o'clock when he pulled into a small library and hopped out. He went immediately to the reference section and looked at a phone book that was two years out of date.

When he found Gideon's name and address he jotted it down on a slip of paper and darted back out the door to the rented Civic. The built in GPS system in the dash of the car was a Godsend; he punched in the address and within moments was driving towards Gideon's house, and hopefully, the end of this terrible, long nightmare.

He was tempted to call his parents in Vancouver and warn them, but, warn them of what, he wondered? Should he warn them that men were going to come and kill them? Should he warn them that those men were going to kill them because he had refused to stay quiet? Should he tell them about the deal that he had made with the devil?

Randle Pulled onto the street that Gideon's house was supposedly on and slowed down to a crawl as he scanned the addresses. When he found the right one, he saw the blue car in the drive and smiled, looked like he was home.

Sara pulled up to Gideon's house turned off the car, staring at the door. The message from Gideon had been a shock, and Sara had wracked her brain trying to figure out what she could do. In the end the only thing she could think of was to pick up Gideon's mail, and maybe it would help keep his house looking normal. A late 50's looking oriental man was standing at Gideon's door, he turned as Sara got out of the car.

"Do you know where Gideon is?" he asked.

Sara shook her head, suddenly remembering what Gideon had said about the people that had murdered Kieran. They might come after him. "I don't know." she said, trying to put on a straight face.

"I'm his old Commanding Officer." the man on the porch said. "I really do need to find him, it's very important."

"I don't know where he is." Sara said with a smile. "I'm sorry."

Randle seemed to get confused for a moment. "I have some very important information that Gideon needs," Randle stepped forward and Sara jumped back towards her car. Randle quickly composed himself. "I'm sorry; it's been a stressful day."

Sara nodded. "I can see that."

"My name is Colonel Randle Yim." Randle said and held out his hand, Sara took it tentatively. "Can you get a message to him, if he contacts you?"

"I'll let him know you're looking for him."

"No!" Randle exclaimed, then calmed again. "Let him know that I'm here and I want in from the cold."

Sara looked confused for a moment, stepped pass Randle to get Gideon's mail. "That's a strange message."

"He'll know what it means," Randle said as he headed back to his car.

*

Gideon had just relieved Jim in the club chair and was munching on a turkey sandwich that he had made in the small kitchen. He had just finished with a chapter of Psalms when Kyle Dowdy shuffled into the kitchen and poured a cup of strong, black coffee. He wandered into the living room and sat down across from Gideon.

Gideon set the Bible into his lap and studied the man. His eyes were bloodshot and dark circles were under his eyes, making them look sunken and deep set into his skull. His hair was brown, and thinning on the top, despite the fact that Gideon could only guess that he was in his early thirties. Kyle still sat straight in his club chair, even though he must have still been exhausted. Gideon smiled, this man had confidence, and drive.

Kyle smiled, causing wrinkles around his brown eyes. "How'd you sleep?"

Gideon shrugged. "Slept better, slept worse."

"I can imagine." He sipped his coffee and looked towards the curtains, which covered a large bay window. "Wish we could open those and let some light in." he sighed.

One of the officers from the card game in the kitchen came in, and handed Kyle a cell phone. "Call for you, Inspector."

Kyle took the phone with a nod and held it to his ear. "Dowdy."

"Kyle, its Greg Driver." Kyle sighed at the sound of his boss. "We've another homicide up here in Ottawa. I've assigned it to Peters, but I think it may have some connection with what you and Giles are working on."

"Have you had a chance to read Giles' report?" Kyle asked. "I don't think we can afford any more connections with this thing."

"In the report Giles said that Jim Barris had gone to see his old commanding officer, Randle Yim."

"Yeah, he didn't get anything from him, though." Kyle said, taking another sip of coffee.

"He was attacked in his apartment this morning." Driver said. "He killed two men, presumably in self defense, now he's in the wind."

140

Kyle sighed. "Do you have IDs on the bodies?"

Kyle heard the shuffling of papers. "Sergeant Greg Evens and Corporal Martin Mays, those names mean anything to you?"

"Gideon and Jim both said that one of the fake CISD agents that approached them was named Greg Evens." Kyle said. "Could be a coincidence."

"We're the RCMP." Driver muttered. "We don't believe in coincidences."

"Can you get Peters to dig into Evens' background?" Kyle asked.

"I'll point him that way right now." Driver said before he hung up the phone.

When Kyle handed the cell back to the officer, he noticed Gideon staring calmly at him. Kyle knew what he wanted so he related the conversation to him over a couple minutes. Gideon sat back in his chair and smiled.

"Well that solves the mystery of the CISD agents." He said. "It was just the bad guys trying to do some damage control. If they had found the file, then this whole thing would have been buried and no one would be any the wiser for it."

"But why try to kill Yim?" Kyle asked.

Gideon sighed. "He must know something that we don't. Maybe he found something out? He works for George Barkley as his special operations liaison."

"We need to find him before they do." Kyle said, and got up to make himself another coffee. He stayed in the kitchen and used the cell phone that he had talked with Driver on to contact Peters, the RCMP Investigator in Ottawa that was working the Yim case.

Gideon went back to his reading another chapter of Psalms and a few chapters of John before he went back to his room to call Sara on her cell. He lay down and dialed the number, waiting patiently as it rang and smiled at the sound of her voice.

"Hello?"

"Told you I was safe." He quipped.

"Gideon!" she cried. "Where are you?"

"I can't tell you that. It's a safe house for the RCMP." Gideon paused, needing the conversation to somehow be normal. "Tell me about your day."

"I will, but first I need to tell you about the man I met today." Gideon's heart sank a little. "I was getting your mail and a man was looking for you there."

"Are you alright?" Gideon suddenly asked.

"I'm fine," Sara replied. "He said his name was Randle Yim, and he wanted you to know that he's here and wants to come in from the cold."

Gideon was shocked. He sat up suddenly and asked, "Where is he now?"

"I don't know. He got in his car and drove away."

"What kind of car?"

"A blue Honda Civic." Sara replied. "It had a rental bumper sticker."

"Hold on." Gideon said. "This is very important, and I need you to talk to one of the Mounties here."

Gideon jumped up and rushed to the kitchen.

"Kyle, you're never going to believe this." He said. "I know where Colonel Yim is. Well, at least I know how to find him."

SEVEN

Colonel Randle Yim lay on the bed of the small, cheap hotel in Kitchener, ON. He stared at the ceiling and tried not to think about what was going on around him. He really should have been going to sleep, it was nearing midnight, but sleep wouldn't come for him. He had abandoned his home, was wanted by the most powerful people in the country and he had information that would bring all of those people down. He was a dead man; he just wasn't ready to give up yet.

He went over the counter measures he had taken to get to this hotel. The room and the car that he drove in were under an assumed name. He had asked for a corner room on the first floor to give him better options to escape, should the need arise. He had not unpacked anything from the gym bag that he carried and he was planning to sleep in his clothes, and even planned to leave his shoes on.

His mind wandered to Gideon, the best soldier he had ever known, he followed orders, rarely questioning those orders and worked himself into the perfect fighting machine. He had acquired two or three black belts in various martial arts and had become a deadly knife fighter as well as a brilliant tactician. It was that tactical brilliance that Randle was hoping for now, he was grasping at the small straws that said that Gideon could figure a way out of this.

His heart went cold, but Gideon had been diagnosed with PTSD a couple years ago. Would his mind be able to think clearly enough to plan an escape for him? He was aware that Doneven and Barkley both knew of Gideon's involvement, were they putting pressure on Gideon, just as they had with him? He knew that they had ordered the execution of Kieran James, Doneven's old Chief of Staff, and had ordered Randle himself to set up surveillance on Gideon. Was Gideon going to be able to talk, let alone plan?

He took a deep breath and slowly let it out, realizing that worrying about this was useless. He had played his last card. Connecting with Gideon and, perhaps, talking to the RCMP officers that he knew were now involved. Randle smiled at the tone of Patricks' voice when he had mentioned that officer Dowdy had visited him was priceless. Patricks, who was known for his lack of emotion was almost screaming at Randle to get some kind of information to him. He had done his part, but the surveillance information was all but useless. Everyone knew that Gideon and Kieran James would be questioned, and even that the reporter, Jerry Price who had broken the story in some small town rag, would get a visit from the famous Canadian Police Force.

Randle's heart nearly burst from his chest when his phone rang. Scrambling forward he pulled it off the bedside table and spoke, "Hello," he said, forcing his voice to sound calm.

"Hello, sir." Randle recognized Gideon's deep voice almost immediately. "I understand you'd like to get out of the cold."

"I'm sorry you must have the wrong room." Randle replied, his suspicion getting the better of him.

"Sir," Gideon continued. "There are only two other living people who know what happened in that small village outside Moghedishu. You and Jim Barris, shall I relate the story so you can confirm it's me?"

"Just tell me how many were dead." Randle said, his mouth going dry.

"Forty-seven," Gideon replied, his voice going soft and regretful.

"She got the message to you." Randle said, relief flooding into his body he flopped back onto the bed. Then he sat up straight again. "How did you get this number?"

"A little help from my friends." Gideon replied. "I'm being kept safe by the RCMP."

"If you can find me," Randle said standing and grabbing his gym bag. "They can find me to."

"Sir," Gideon almost yelled to get Randle's attention. "Right outside your door is an RCMP Inspector named John Giles. He'll wait there until you're ready to leave. He'll bring you to me, to where it's safe." Gideon's voice was calm and soothing; Randle felt the tension ease a little.

"They can find me." Randle muttered softly.

*

At the safe house, Gideon was sitting in a chair at the small kitchen table, talking quietly to Randle. It was decided to use Gideon to speak with Randle Yim, because he had had a good working relationship with him when they served together. Gideon's hands were sweaty and he was hunched over the tabletop, staring down at the pale blue Formica design. Jim and Kyle were listening in on earphones and an IT guy was working at a laptop computer to ensure that the conversation was being recorded and secure.

"He's losing it," Kyle said softly.

"He'll be fine," Jim said, glancing over at Kyle. "He's been in tighter situations."

"They can find my parents." Randle said through the earphones.

"We can bring them in too." Gideon said softly, trying to ignore Jim's and Kyle's voices.

Kyle looked over at two officers sitting in the living room at two more computers monitoring the situation at the hotel, one in communication with Giles, the other watching the area from satellite coverage. He snapped his fingers, "Find his parents." One of the officers started typing at his laptop.

Gideon glanced up at Kyle. "We're working on getting them safe now, sir." Kyle nodded.

Randle was silent on the phone. Gideon could hear him pacing back and forth. It sounded like he walked into the bathroom and then back out into the main area. He could hear subtle rustling as he moved the curtain to look outside.

"What's Giles look like?" Randle asked.

"About 6'4", white, brown hair," Gideon said. "Pretty solid guy, could have been a decent linebacker."

"Call him."

Kyle pulled out his phone and dialed Giles. A moment later Giles answered.

"Giles."

"He asked us to call you." Kyle said. "Stay on the line."

Kyle looked at Gideon, who was staring at the table top.

*

Randle watched as the man outside his door answered the phone. He spoke briefly then stood there with it to his ear.

"Tell him to take two steps back." Randle said.

A second later the man took two steps back.

"Is he armed?" Randle asked.

"Yes, sir," Gideon replied.

"Tell him to open his trunk and then open all four doors of his car and leave them open." Randle hitched the gym bag up onto his shoulder, watching through a small crack in the corner of the curtain. Once the man had opened the trunk and doors he said, "Tell him to remove the magazine and the slide from his firearm and place the slide in the trunk, the weapon in the back seat and the magazine on the passenger seat."

Randle watched as the man removed his weapon and dismantled it, as per Randle's instructions. "Now tell him to get into the driver's side of the car, put his seatbelt on and place the keys on the dash. Then place both hands on the wheel."

The man moved slowly and deliberately, not using any movements to startle Randle. When he was in the car and his hands on the wheel, Randle said. "I'm coming in."

Randle opened the door and casually walked out towards the car. His heart was pounding and his eyes were constantly moving around him, searching for danger. He placed his bag in the trunk and noted the slide from a Glock 9 lying in the corner. Moving up to the driver's rear door he noted the rest of the Glock on the back seat. He closed the driver's door, and then the door behind it. Moving around the rear of the car he closed the passenger side back door and then got into the passenger seat. Randle leaned over, took the keys and started the car.

"You can start driving now, Constable Jones." Randle said, sitting sideways in the car, facing the man.

"My name is Inspector John Giles," the man said. "Paranoid much?"

Randle finally released a sigh that had been building in his chest since that morning. "I've had a bad day."

*

After Randle said he was coming in, Gideon hung up the phone and let his head rest on the table. Jim walked around him and patted him on the back, leaving his hand there for a moment after the last pat.

"I'm going lay down," he said. "Kyle, can you let me know when the Colonel gets here?"

"No problem." Kyle replied.

Gideon needed to decompress. His heart was still racing and his stomach felt like he would throw up the pasta and canned sauce they'd had for dinner. He stood and walked woodenly into his room, crashing down on the bed and reached for the phone.

He needed to talk to someone, have a normal conversation, something that didn't involve people dying, or wanting to kill him. He needed to hear Sara's voice. Just hear her say anything and he knew he'd feel better.

The phone rang once, twice, and then a third time before Sara answered.

"We brought him in from the cold." Gideon said after she said hello. "Sorry for calling so late."

"I just got home from work a few minutes ago. Is this going to take much longer?" Sara asked.

"No," Gideon said with a sigh. "How was your day? I need to hear about it."

"Oh, you know, the usual," Sara laughed, knowing that it was what Gideon needed. "Band-Aids and medication, the life of a nurse is so glamorous." She paused. "I did get an e-mail from John Rogers. He's quite upset that you didn't make your meeting this morning to go over the budget for the camping trip."

"Tell him I've been busy." Gideon said, a smile starting to form on his face. His heart had slowed down the moment he heard Sara's voice, or maybe it was because he'd lain on the bed. He didn't care, he was starting to feel better and that's what mattered.

"I sent him a reply and said you were probably just out on a bender with your army buddies." Sara laughed.

Gideon laughed too, the first he could remember in he didn't know how long. "That'll go over well." He thought for a moment. "There's an extra key for my house under the big rock in the front garden. The budget for John is in a folder on my bedside table."

"I'll swing over in the morning on my way to work." Sara worked twelve hour shifts, starting at eleven. "Call me again tomorrow?"

"It's a date." Gideon said, his heart thumping at using the 'date' word.

"Well," Sara said and Gideon could hear the smile in her voice. "You certainly know how to show a girl an exciting time."

They said goodbye and Gideon laid his head back and smiled. He'd try to get a few minutes of sleep before Giles got back with Colonel Yim in a moment; he just wanted to enjoy the warm feeling growing in his chest first.

*

Randle was still facing Giles in the front seat of the car. Giles was facing forward, both hands on the wheel and concentrating on driving the car.

"How did you find me?" Randle asked.

"The woman you talked to noticed the colour, and make of the car, and the rental sticker on the bumper." Giles explained. "We ran your name through the rental agencies and when that came up as a dead end we asked about oriental men renting blue Honda Civics this morning."

"And Gideon confirmed my picture on the driver's license I used." Randle said. "Clever."

"Not my first rodeo." Giles smiled. "Then it was just a matter of running your fake name through hotel registries in the area."

"But the motel I was at didn't use computers, and I paid in cash."

"You still had to show ID." Giles said. "After the computer search came up blank, we started calling the smaller motels."

"Clever." Randle said again.

"We ran a search on train tickets too, found the ticket in your name." Giles said. "We know you were in town when someone shot at you."

"I was in my kitchen." Randle replied. "They're cleaning house."

"What did you find out that you shouldn't have?" Giles said casually, hoping to keep Randle at ease.

Randle huffed out a laugh. "I didn't find out anything. I was a part of it."

Giles was silent for a moment, staring ahead, trying to look calm. If this man was really a part of this huge conspiracy, then he might be in trouble. His Glock was in three pieces scattered around the car, and the man across from him was a trained killer, having worked in Special Operations for years, just that morning he had killed two men!

"Are my parents safe?" Randle asked.

"I. . ." Giles stammered, and then checked himself. "We can check once we get to the safe house."

The thought suddenly occurred to Giles. Was this man being sent in specifically to kill Gideon and Jim? Was he bringing in the assassin to do the job? Giles had no idea if Randle had any weapons on him, or in the bag that he had placed in the trunk. He darted a look at Randle and quickly examined him again. He had made a cursory observation when he was walking around the car, but now he focused on his waist and under the arms, where a firearm would be kept.

"I'm not armed." Randle said. "And I'm not the enemy."

"That's a statement I would expect from the enemy." Giles said dryly.

Randle huffed out another laugh. "My parents were threatened if I didn't help. They came to Canada shortly before I was born from China. They were so proud when I was accepted to the Royal Military College in Kingston." Randle paused allowing himself a smile from the memory. "Just before the Dawson mission, I was approached and told that if I didn't ask any questions my parents would be safe."

Giles nodded, understanding the desire to keep his parents safe now. "And once they had you?"

Randle nodded. "They had me. I moved equipment for them, arranged intelligence missions, passed on classified information, and even arranged for their men to be placed on the rosters for mission they wouldn't normally be available for."

"Wait a minute," Giles said suddenly. "All this was put in place for the Dawson mission?"

Randle was confused for a moment. "You don't understand, do you?" He laughed loudly, a full bellied laugh that went on for a few seconds. "This has been going on for years! These people, whom I will name once my parents are safe, have been hiring out Canadian soldiers and equipment as mercenaries, all the overhead financed through the military budget and all the payment going to their pockets."

Giles pressed down on the gas a little more.

EIGHT

Colonel Patricks finished moving the last of the money from his European accounts to the one account in the Cayman Islands, under the alias Ronald Woods. He then started a program which would wipe his entire hard drive, and then cover it with random letters and numbers seven times, ensuring that the data would be lost forever. Being as careful as he was, he also intended to take a sledge hammer to it once that was done, and maybe dumping the remains in the Rideau Canal.

He picked up an envelope with all of the necessary IDs for "Ronald Woods", including a passport, and threw another envelope with his entire ID for Colonel David Patricks into the fireplace. He soaked it with lighter fluid and then set it ablaze. He stood for a moment watching his identity being destroyed. He thought that he should feel something at the moment, some kind of regret, but instead he just felt . . . nothing.

The LED TV in the corner was running the latest news story about a training mission that had gone horribly wrong, four Canadian Soldiers with the Canadian Special Operations Regiment were dead in an accident caused by a claymore mine that had unexpectedly exploded in training manoeuvres. Patricks smiled, four more loose ends tied up. He placed the new ID in the inside jacket pocket of the grey suit he was wearing and sighed. A shame that they weren't able to find Yim, if he had been silenced then the escape from Canada might not have been necessary.

He had advised the six remaining soldiers under him and both Doneven and Barkley to leave the country via their false identities too, but for Doneven and Barkley that would be slightly more difficult, given their positions in the government. He knew it would take an hour or more for the erasing program to finish running, so he opened a bottle of Glen Livet and sat down to watch his handiwork on the news.

Doneven had been the first to mention the idea in passing at a party for Patricks' commanding officer at the time. He had made the comment as a joke, but was impressed when Patricks laid out a series of logistical possibilities where using the Canadian Military as a mercenary force was possible.

151

His commanding officer laughed and told him to forget the plans, but a week later Doneven contacted him and invited him to dinner at his home. When he arrived he was surprised to find that the Minister of Defense at the time, Lewis Wood, was also there. The three of them planned late into the night and by the end of the week, Patricks' plan was in motion.

*

Chris Taylor woke and fumbled around to grab the ringing phone from his bed side table. His wife, Tina, turned her back to him with a loud sigh. Chris paused a moment to look at her, concerned before saying hello into the phone.

"Pastor?" The voice on the other end was instantly recognized as Mrs. Dunn, an elderly lady from the church who had taken in Fred Cross. "It's Ella. Fred hasn't come back yet. He went home to pick up some things, but he still hasn't come back. I'm more than a little bit worried."

"Have you called Fred's parents' house?" Chris asked.

"Of course," Ella replied. "There was no answer."

Chris started to roll out of bed. "I'll swing by and see what's up." He hung up the phone and turned to his wife.

"Just be careful." Tina said without turning over.

"I will be." Chris leaned over and kissed her blond head.

Chris drove the four kilometers from his suburban neighborhood to the run down area of poorly kept houses and rows of provincial operated townhouses. When he arrived at the Cross house, a two bedroom bungalow with sagging gutters and peeling blue paint, he was surprised to see the front door open. He waited for a moment, expecting to see Fred walk out the door with a bag or two.

When no one exited the house he turned the engine of his blue caravan off and stepped onto the street. He chuckled as he closed the door; he was wearing white Nikes and blue pajama pants, along with his Savior Bible College t-shirt.

Approaching the front door, Chris spotted a skinny, matted cat sniffing around the open door. Somewhere off to his right a dog barked and someone swore at it to be quiet.

That's when he saw the flash and heard the gunshot from inside the Cross house.

*

Colonel Randle Yim was sitting at the kitchen table in the safe house. His head was hanging between his shoulders and his elbows were resting on the cheap surface. an untouched mug of coffee was next to his right elbow.

John Giles was standing beside him, listening to his cell phone. A tech guy was setting up a video camera across from Yim and a microphone, connected to a laptop was on a holder in front of his bowed head.

Gideon Steele and Jim Barris were in the living room of the safe house, each lost in their own memories of the man that had lead them for so many years during their time in the military. Kyle Dowdy was in the living room as well, pacing back and forth, talking to a Crown Attorney in Ottawa, having woken him at home a few minutes after Yim had arrived.

Giles took his phone away from his ear and held it towards Yim. "We have your parents, they're safe in Vancouver." he said with a smile. "Would you like to speak with them?"

Yim's head shot up and he grabbed the phone from Giles, quickly speaking in Chinese. After a brief conversation he handed the phone back to Giles and softly thanked him.

Giles smiled and snapped his fingers at Kyle, who told the CA on his phone they were ready. The two men sat down across from Yim, one on each side of the camera and, as Kyle put his phone on speaker he placed it on the table. The same tech guy that had set up the camera plugged the phone into a charger and silently went to his laptop.

Giles smiled gently to Yim. "Are you ready?"

Yim nodded.

"On the phone we have David Gramecy, a Crown Attorney from Ottawa." Kyle said softly.

"Hello, sir" Yim said woodenly.

"Are we recording yet?" Gramecy said, his voice tinny and far away, from the phone. When Giles said no, Gramecy continued, "I'd like to thank you for coming forward Colonel, and if this is as big as everyone is telling me, then we can certainly make a deal to keep you out of prison, but I need to inform you that military law has been broken as well, and I have no authority there. Are you sure you don't want a military lawyer present before we begin?"

"Start recording." Yim said, straightening his back, and causing Gideon and Jim to smile, seeing their old commander coming out.

The tech pressed a button on the laptop and Giles said, "Recording."

"My name is David Gramecy. I am a Crown Attorney working out of Ottawa, Ontario, Canada. I am currently conferencing via phone to oversee questioning of Colonel Randle Yim of the Canadian Special Operations Regiment Command. Colonel Yim is currently stationed at Parliament Hill as the Special Operations liaison for the Minister of Defense. Colonel Yim has waived his right for both civil and military counsel during this questioning. Colonel Yim is also aware that he may halt questioning at any time to acquire counsel. Do you understand those statements, Colonel?"

"I do."

"The questioning is being held in an undisclosed location due to an attempt on Colonel Yim's life earlier this morning. Also present at this meeting are RCMP Investigators, John Giles and Kyle Dowdy. At this time I shall hand control of the questioning to the RCMP." Gramecy went quiet and the sound of shuffling papers were heard as he prepared to take notes.

"This is RCMP Sergeant Inspector John Giles, can I get you anything to drink or eat, Colonel?"

"No thank you."

"Why don't we start with the names of the people involved in the conspiracy to use Canadian Military personnel and equipment in mercenary actions." Giles said, wanting to get names on the record as quickly as possible.

"Governor General Doneven and the Minister of Defense Barkley are the leading decision makers." Yim said clearly. "The leading tactician for the movement of military personnel and equipment, as well as the operational tactics and planning is Colonel David Patricks, formerly of Canadian Special Operations Regiment Command, but recently posted to the Special Records facility in Ottawa to try to ease the damage by the missing records for Operation B-2425."

"Can you tell us more about that mission?" Giles said. "B-2425."

Yim nodded, stealing a glance at Gideon and Jim. "I was approached early March, of 2003, by then Lieutenant Colonel Patricks."

After four hours of talking, Yim's mouth was dry and his voice scratchy. Giles sat back and rubbed his eyes, shaking his head. The technician switched off the recorder and said, "We're off."

Giles leaned back and looked at Kyle with a big grin. "We've got them."

*

Particks stayed in a hotel that night under his assumed name. Early the next morning, just before the sun rose he made his way out of the shabby building to a waiting cab that he had called earlier. He casually dropped his luggage into the trunk and started to get into the back seat. Within moments he was on his way to the MacDonald Cartier International Airport.

*

Minister of Defense Barkley was getting into the back of the Black Lincoln Town car and smiled at his aide. Donald Preston was looking like he was sick. His eyes were wide and his face was slightly pale. Sweat gleamed on his high forehead that was going prematurely bald.

"Something wrong, Donald?" Barkley started to open his briefcase to go over the day's schedule.

"No, sir," Donald replied softly.

One of the RCMP security officers assigned to him turned around to face him from the front seat. "Everything's fine, sir," he said with a smile.

Donald's door opened and another RCMP officer pulled Donald out and got in beside Barkley. "You won't need your schedule today, sir," the officer said. "You'll be busy for the entire day."

*

Governor General Doneven was sitting at his desk. His eyes were red and bloodshot, dark bags had formed under them and he blinked constantly. His stomach roiled and he kept a bottle of Pepto Bismol on the left corner of the large, oak surface.

He nearly jumped out of his skin when a loud rap sounded on his door. He hadn't left his office all night after the call from Patricks, and he hadn't slept either. He was busy collecting reams and reams of paper, anything that might be used against him in court, anything that could connect him in any small way to Barkley and Patricks. The result was sitting in front of the leather couch on the coffee table, four large banker's boxes, all filled with documents, orders and operational planning reports. All as good as full color video and a smoking gun.

The door opened and two RCMP security detail officers walked in. Doneven had known them for a few years, they worked security on the grounds and buildings of The House of Commons, but he didn't know them

155

well.

One of the men eyed the boxes on the coffee table and smiled. "All packed up and ready to go, sir?"

Doneven looked down at the surface of his desk and wept.

*

"We're going to have to take you in for a bit," Giles said to Yim as they got in the back seat of Kyle's car. "Won't be for long, the crown attorney said."

Yim nodded. "Guess my military career is over."

Gideon shrugged. "Maybe not, sir. Maybe they'll tack this up to coercion on Doneven and Barkley's part."

Yim laughed. "Coercion. Yeah that'll help me move up the military ladder."

"I think now you've got to just hope to hold on to the rung you have, sir," Gideon replied.

Yim nodded. "Maybe so."

They drove to the county jail and Gideon and Jim stayed with Yim as long as they were allowed to, then they hitched a ride back to the Gideon's house with Giles.

On the way, Gideon's phone chirped. It was a text message from Chris Taylor. It was just a couple words. "Need you"

Gideon showed the phone to Jim, who shrugged. "Pretty vague," he intoned in a deep voice.

"What is it?" Giles pulled in beside Gideon's car. He showed the RCMP officer his phone. "Where is he?"

Gideon tapped a message into the phone and got an almost immediate reply. "He's at the police station," he said after reading it.

Giles put the car in reverse and drove them down the tree lined streets to the station, all the men were silent, each wondering why the small, thin pastor would be there, but none of them asked the question, knowing that no one in the car knew the answer.

When they walked in, Chris was sitting in a plastic chair in the waiting area, he took a long look at Giles, who smiled.

"Hello, pastor," Giles said with a smile, he held his hand out.

"Hello," Chris said, taking the man's hand. "I'm sorry I forget your name."

"James Giles," Giles said.

After a brief description of where the two men had met for Gideon and Jim's benefit, Chris turned to Gideon. "Last night, Ella Dunn called me, the lady that took Fred Cross in, she was worried because Fred hadn't come back from picking up some things at his parents' house.

"I went there and before I even got to the door someone started shooting in the house. I ran back to my van and called 911, but then three people came out of the house with Fred and threw him in a car and drove off."

Gideon frowned. "The shots?"

Chris' eyes started to fill with tears. "Fred's mom was dead inside the house. The police asked me to identify the body while we were there."

Giles shook his head. "They're pretty short staffed here, eh?"

Gideon nodded. "Yeah, why?"

"If they had more time or resources they wouldn't have brought Pastor Chris into an active crime scene to ID a body. They probably would have spent the time to check fingerprints or the ownership of the house and stuff back at the morgue," Giles explained.

"What can we do?" Jim stepped forward, his massive bulk comforting to the smaller pastor.

"I don't know," Chris said. "The police won't tell me anything and I'm worried about Fred."

Giles nodded. "You should be," he muttered, looking around at the small station. "I need to head to the RCMP detachment here for a few hours. Can you hitch a ride back with Pastor Chris?" he asked Gideon and Jim.

"No problem," Gideon replied.

An hour and a half later Giles signed his name to the bottom of a form and handed it to the RCMP detachment Commander. The slightly overweight man with the classic "police" mustache smiled at him.

"Don't know why you want to do this," he said. "But I'm not going to complain, given your recent arrests here and in Ottawa."

"I see an opportunity to do some good here, sir," Giles replied.

The Commander nodded and signed on a line next to Giles' signature. "I'll call your detachment commander today and we'll get it all worked out. We may even be able to arrange for you to start here next Monday."

"Thank you, sir."

The Commander placed the transfer request in his outbox.

NINE

Fred looked up from the bed he was sitting on. His left eye was blackened and almost swollen shut. He was pretty sure his nose was broken and one of his ribs was cracked. He was used to pain like this, though. For most of his young life his father, he couldn't think of him as his Dad, had beaten him.

His father was a drug dealer and a drug addict. Over the last few months when he had moved into Mrs. Dunn's house his father had gotten even more erratic. Smoking more crack than he sold, and getting farther and farther in debt with the suppliers that provided him with drugs.

Guess the suppliers had gotten tired of losing money.

He leaned back against the cheap paneling nailed to the wall. The bed was dirty and stained, he must have been in another crack house. There were no windows in the room and he assumed he was in a basement room provided for "customers". His father had a few in the basement of the house Fred had grown up in.

No, not grown up, survived.

Fred got up and went to the door, listening briefly before he tried the handle. It was locked. He went back to the bed and sat down. It was a small room, only a few paces wide and scarcely more long. A single bed was the only piece of furniture in it. The walls were bare, covered in cheap paneling that made it look like a recreation room from the seventies. The carpet was threadbare and maybe once had been cream colored but now was stained dark grey, he shuddered to think of the last time it was cleaned.

Fred Cross bowed his head and prayed.

TEN

Gideon and Jim sat on the front porch drinking tea from delicate china tea cups. Neither of them said anything, merely staring out at the darkening evening sky.

Jim had called Sara to let her know he was safe, she seemed relieved, but resigned to his call and that bothered him. He really liked her and wanted her to like him, but he was worried that his past would somehow get in the way.

Jim had checked in on his sheep operation in Quebec and was pleased to learn that it would be a good year.

"Maybe I should take more extended vacations," he quipped in French on the phone.

They sat, finished their teas and Gideon filled the cups again from the china pot between them.

"What now, Cap?" Jim asked, breaking the silence.

"We move on, I guess," Gideon replied, waving at Mrs. Gable as she stepped out to examine her pristine garden.

"To what?"

"We still have to arrange the youth survival retreat," Gideon said.

"You think the church is really going to let that move forward after all this?"

"Don't know what they're going to do, so until I know, I'm going to move forward like everything is going according to plan," Gideon said with a smile. "Just like in the Forces."

Jim smiled back, somewhat wryly. "And just like in the Forces we have no clue what the plan is, who's making it, or what the final outcome is going to be."

"God is in control," Gideon said.

"Glad someone is," Jim muttered.

They sat in silence a little longer. "I'm worried about Fred," Gideon said, interrupting the silence.

"You'd be silly not to be."

"I wonder if there's some way we could help." Gideon turned his head slightly and regarded Jim from the corner of his eye.

Jim sat as if he hadn't heard him and sipped at his tea. After about five minutes he said, "So do I."

THE END

Coming Soon!

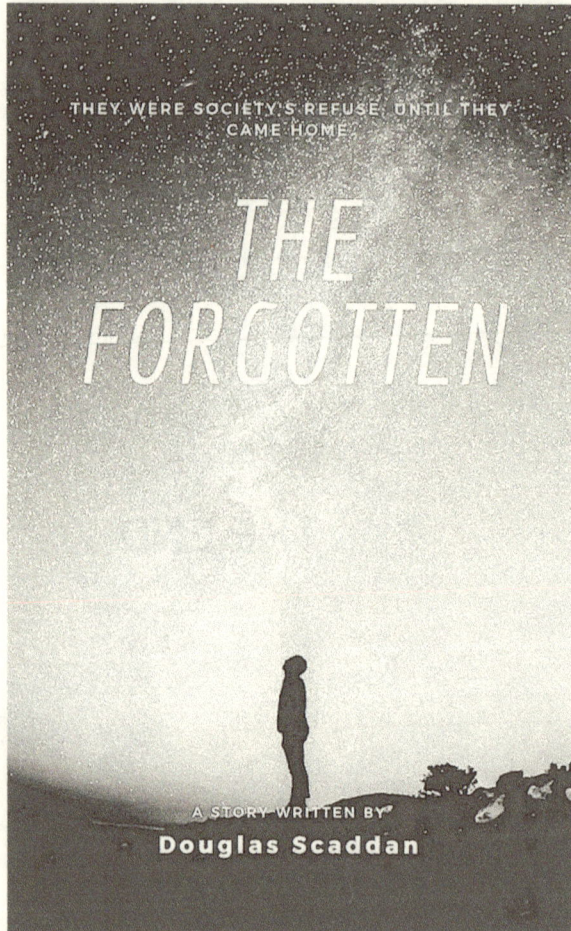

THEY WERE SOCIETY'S REFUSE, UNTIL THEY CAME HOME

THE FORGOTTEN

A STORY WRITTEN BY

Douglas Scaddan

Summer 2020!

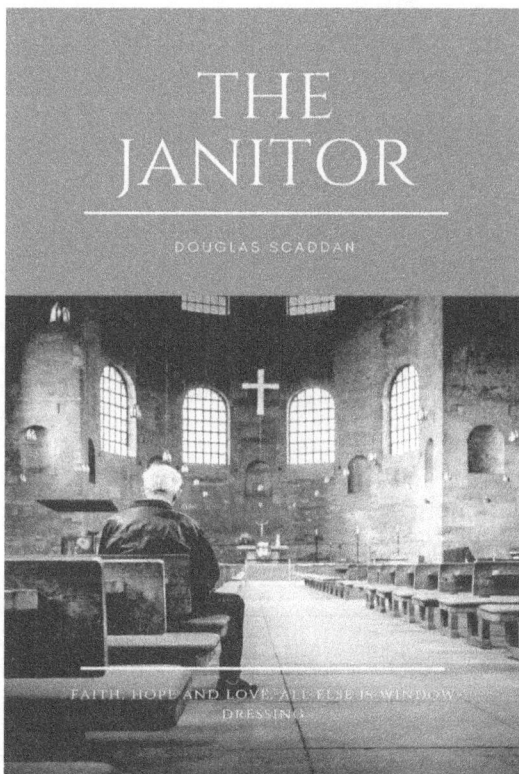

About The Author

Douglas Scaddan lives in Kitchener, Ontario, Canada. He is a Developmental Service Worker for Christian Horizons, a non profit organization that is dedicated to serving people with exceptional needs.

He loves his job.

He enjoys writing about things that have meaning and maybe a little bit of controversy in them. His Soldiers of God series explores the needs of soldiers that return from service with problems they never even knew they had.

He enjoys reading, writing and working out. The latter he sometimes finds difficult to gather motivation for.

www.ingramcontent.com/pod-product-compliance
Lightning Source LLC
LaVergne TN
LVHW091256080426
835510LV00007B/284